DREAMS AND HEALING

by

John A. Sanford

Paulist Press
New York/ Ramsey/ Toronto

Library of Congress
Catalog Card Number: 78-61723

ISBN: 0-8091-2129-8

Published by Paulist Press
Editorial Office: 1865 Broadway, New York, N.Y. 10023
Business Office: 545 Island Road, Ramsey, N.J. 07446

Printed and bound in the
United States of America

DREAMS AND HEALING

CONTENTS

ACKNOWLEDGMENTS

I am greatly indebted to the many people who allowed me to use their dreams for illustrative material in this book, and without whom this book would not be possible, and especially to the young man and woman whose dreams make up two sections of this volume. In all cases, their material has been presented exactly as it occurred, except for some unimportant changes that were made in order to preserve anonymity. Of course, no actual names have been used.

I am also greatly indebted to my friend and colleague, the Rev. Morton T. Kelsey, who first called my attention to the interesting series of dreams which make up "Martin's Dreams," and to my wife, Linny, and my secretary, Helen Macey, who gave me invaluable help in the preparation of this manuscript.

INTRODUCTION

A friend of mine, the Rev. Richard D. Thomson, tells the true story of Patillo Higgins, a one-armed gunsmith who became obsessed with the idea that a great pool of oil lay beneath a swamp outside of Beaumont, Texas. In spite of the derision with which he met, Higgins was able to finance an extensive search for the hidden oil, but for many years the only thing his drilling rigs produced were debts, water, and quicksand. But Patillo was not easily discouraged. He tried again and again for several more years until he was completely out of money and the butt of jokes of others around him. Still he did not give up. He found one more financial backer and made one more attempt in the face of ridicule and scorn and, finally, in 1901, he met with success. After nearly twenty years, Patillo Higgins struck oil in the form of a gigantic gusher that shot a black stream of oil hundreds of feet into the air. It proved to be the largest oil discovery in the world at that time, and made Higgins a wealthy man.

It is something like this with the unconscious. Most people think the soul of man contains nothing but quicksand and emptiness, even though Jesus once declared, "The kingdom of God is within you."[1] But for a person who is persistent, and who continues to explore the depths and heights of his own soul, there is a great wealth awaiting him.

Dreams are like a gusher of oil from our inner depths. It

---

[1] Luke 17:21 KJV.

1

was in 1966 that my first book on dreams[2] was published, and at that time it was a rare thing for a book to be published on this subject. Today there is a gradually growing interest in the subject of dreams, and for a long time I have felt the need for another book, more detailed and comprehensive than my first one. This book is divided into three sections. The first section is a general introduction to the subject. It contains some of the same ideas that are in my first book, though in many important respects it goes beyond it. The second section contains a series of eight dreams which came to a young university student. At the time this young man had these dreams he was not in any kind of therapy, nor had he ever studied psychology. The most he knew about dreams was from a humanities course he had taken in which he had read Jung's autobiography, *Memories, Dreams, Reflections*. He recalled that he didn't finish this book at the time, that it seemed to be over his head, but he was sufficiently intrigued by what the book had to say about dreams that he wrote down the vivid dreams that came to him, the dreams that make up Part Two.

The dreams in this series are a helpful instrument for teaching because of their great clarity and impact, and because they are not part of a "case history," but come out of the setting of ordinary life. There is also a little story that runs along with these dreams, which enables us to see how the inner events of our dreams fit into the outer events of our lives. The dreams of this young man also resulted in a reawakening of his religious life, which makes them especially helpful to us, for in this day and age many people have difficulty in finding a spiritual life, and this is one area in which dreams can be most helpful.

I might add that I have never met this young man, and, when I first studied his dreams, had little personal knowledge of him. However, we have subsequently corresponded extensively about the dreams. From time to time, in addition to my own discussion of the dreams, I have added his

---

[2]John A. Sanford, *Dreams: God's Forgotten Language*, J.B. Lippincott Co., 1968, (originally published by Rascher Verlag, 1966, as Gottes Vergessene Sprache).

insights and comments. These are in quotation marks because they are taken directly from our correspondence, with his consent, of course.

The third section of the book contains a study of a series of five dreams that came in a span of two weeks to a woman in her early middle-age. In addition to their unusual clarity, I have included these dreams because they show how dreams relate to the life of a woman, just as, in section two, the dreams show how life unfolds in a young man. Dreams and the life of the soul seem to have an unusual interest and meaning for women, who often take to such things more naturally than men. I am grateful to the woman who had these dreams and the young university student for allowing their dreams to be published.

It took Patillo Higgins some twenty years to find his oil. It will not take nearly as long for us to find the unconscious with the aid of our dreams, for the wealth that is locked within us wants to be found and tries to reach consciousness through the medium of the dream. There will, however, be a certain price that we will have to pay if we wish to tap into the creative possibilities of relating to the unconscious, just as Patillo Higgins had to make his initial investment of time, energy, and money. Learning to work with our dreams will require from us time, commitment, and study. Our efforts can be well rewarded, but the fainthearted, or those who want the things of the soul neatly packaged and given to them without cost, will probably not be interested. To those who are in need, and to the strong of heart, the study of dreams and the human soul is a rich field of endeavor, and it is to these people that this book is written.

UNDERSTANDING OUR DREAMS

Our Spiritual Heritage of Dreams

Suppose someone told you that there was something that spoke to you every night, that always presented you with a truth about your own life and soul, that was tailor-made to your individual needs and particular life-story, and that offered to guide you throughout your lifetime and connect you with a source of wisdom far beyond yourself. And, furthermore, suppose that all of this was absolutely free. Naturally you would be astonished that something like this existed. Yet this is exactly the way it is with our dreams.

I clearly remember when my early guide and mentor, Fritz Kunkel, suggested to me that I begin to record my dreams. No one had ever suggested that dreams might be important to me, though by this time I had come in contact with any number of doctors, psychiatrists, ministers and many others in my search for spiritual guidance and psychological wholeness. I was a theological student at the time and had gone through two years of seminary, but no one there had mentioned dreams, nor had the church in which I had been born and raised. But now I was to discover, as I recorded my first dream, that this was the beginning of a lifelong adventure with something like a voice within myself that was going to offer healing and guidance for my life.

I might not have been surprised at Dr. Kunkel's suggestion had I known more of the spiritual life of ancient man, for while dreams are ignored or disparaged in our era, in ancient times they were greatly valued. There is, as far as I

know, no ancient culture in which dreams were not regarded as exceedingly important. The Egyptians, Babylo-
nians, Greeks, and Romans, for instance, all believed
dreams to be an important way in which the soul received
guidance from the spiritual world. Among primitive people
we have many examples of what might be called "dream
cultures," that is, cultures in which dreams are at the center
of a deeply spiritual way of life.

The American Indians are a good example. Dreams,
said Chief Seattle, are given men "in the solemn hours of the
night by the Great Spirit."[1] The soul, it was believed by the
Red Man, is an individual expression of the Great Spirit, but
the soul would wander in darkness unless it received a guiding light. Fortunately, visions and dreams would come from
the Great Spirit to guide the soul. Without such guidance
man's lower nature, which inclines to ignorance, cruelty,
and apathy, would prevail. But the soul enlightened by
dreams can achieve the nobility for which man was created;
he can move forward and reach the source of all learning,
which is the knowledge of God, for, as the Nez Perce Indian
prophet Smohalla said, "Wisdom comes to us in dreams."[2]

The Bible also believed in dreams. It was Abraham Lincoln who once said: "It seems strange how much there is in
the Bible about dreams. There are, I think, some sixteen
chapters in the Old Testament and four or five in the New in
which dreams are mentioned;. . . . If we believe the Bible,
we must accept the fact that, in the old days, God and his
angels came to men in their sleep and made themselves
known in dreams."[3]

We also know that Lincoln believed God *still* spoke to
people in dreams, for he followed his own dreams throughout his life, and has left us a record of some particularly
interesting ones that immediately preceded his death,
which seemed to him to be intimations of the forthcoming
end of his life. But Lincoln was wrong in his statement that

[1]T. C. McCluhan, *Touch the Earth*, Promontory Press, New York, 1971, p. 30.
[2]ibid. p. 56
[3]*The Religion of Lincoln* by William J. Wolf, The Seabury Press, New York, 1963,
p. 29. For other quotations from Lincoln on dreams, see Carl Sandburg's *Abraham
Lincoln, The War Years, Vol. IV*, Harcourt, Brace & World, Inc., 1939, pp. 244-45.

there are some sixteen chapters in the Old Testament on dreams, for in fact dreams, or similar experiences, are recorded or mentioned in almost every part of the Bible from Genesis to Revelation.

The emphasis upon dreams that we find in the Bible is equally prominent in the early church. Every major figure of the early Christian Church through the time of St. Augustine cites dreams as an important way in which God spoke to mankind, and many of the Fathers of the Church wrote psychological treatises on dreams. Tertullian, for instance, went so far as to say, "Beyond a doubt the greater part of mankind derive their knowledge of God from their dreams."[4] A complete study of the dreams in the Bible and the early church would lead us beyond the scope of this book and, besides, it has already been done in my earlier book on dreams, and even more completely in a book by the Rev. Morton T. Kelsey.[5]

Ancient man's belief in dreams gave him a connection to the sources of his spiritual life, but our culture is greatly impoverished in this respect, and a wide gulf has emerged between our conscious life and the life of our souls. Most people today are spiritually stranded, cut off from the living sources of life within. For all of our material well-being, we are a culturally-deprived people, and the energies of the inner man, as though angry at their rejection, take vengeance upon us in the crime, war, and psychological illness which characterize our time.

Anyone who takes human nature seriously must be impressed by the fact that man is a seemingly irrational creature. Human behaviour is *not* reasonable, and mankind acts for all the world as though it was possessed. For ancient man this was an obvious testimony to the reality of the spiritual world that was shown to him in his dreams. Modern man, however, is caught in an attitude of rationalistic materialism, and from this perspective dreams cannot make sense.

---

[4]Tertullian, "*A Treatise on the Soul,*" Ch. XLVII.

[5]Morton T. Kelsey, *God, Dreams, and Revelation,* Augsburg Press, 1974, originally published as *Dreams: The Dark Speech of the Spirit,* Doubleday Company, Inc., 1968.

For this reason our culture leaves dreams out. We are able to persist in our rationalistic materialism because we suffer from the delusion that, while others may be unreasonable, we *are* reasonable. To be sure, we have our disturbed moods and affects, but these, we say are due to what others are doing to us. So we are able to continue believing that only what is logical and rational makes sense, and those things that can be seen, heard, smelled, touched or tasted are real. Dreams make great sense, but it is not logical sense; they are quite real, but they cannot be apprehended by the senses of the body.

We might have been rescued by the church from the adverse affects of this arrogant materialistic philosophy if it were not that the church has reneged on its own spiritual traditions and has succumbed to the rational materialism of our day along with everyone else. For the church, as it became increasingly institutionalized, devalued and denied the reality of the individual soul and its dreams in favor of collectivized creeds, rituals and traditions. In putting the life of the institution above that of the soul, it lost the dream; instead of ministering and listening to the soul, the church sought to mould the individual to the life of the institution. This left the church devoid of its spiritual basis, and open to the same materialism and rationalism that gripped the rest of the world. The church has preferred to ignore the fact that its rejection of dreams went against the views of the Bible and early Christianity.

Now, slowly, a change is coming. In the 20th century the dream is making a comeback as a subject worthy of study and investigation. There is, for instance, the research on sleep and dreaming that has been prevalent since World War II. Careful laboratory studies have shown that everyone dreams about one and a half hours in eight hours of sleep. This can be proven by attaching an electroencephalogram to a sleeping subject. When a certain type of brain wave pattern is discernible, accompanied by rapid eye movement (often referred to as REM sleep) and other physiological changes, the subject is awakened and can usually report dreams. In other types of sleep, dreams are not reported.

Thus we have evidence that everyone dreams, even though many people do not recall their dreams (a point we will discuss later).

It has also been demonstrated that there is a psychological need for REM sleep. Experimenters have deprived subjects of their dreams by wakening them at the onset of REM sleep, or by the use of drugs that have been found to selectively suppress REM sleep. Early experimenters felt that these subjects began to experience anxiety, irritability, and difficulties in concentration. Later experiments did not indicate that deprivation of REM sleep necessarily resulted in serious psychological disturbance, but did show that there was a "REM rebound" effect, that is, persons deprived of REM sleep experienced greatly increased REM sleep when normal sleeping patterns were allowed to resume. This led to speculation that REM sleep might erupt into consciousness if people were deprived of their dream-state sleeping for a sufficiently long period of time. The barrier between the REM sleep and consciousness, however, seems very strong so that eruptions of the REM state into the waking state seldom occur. One significant exception is delerium tremens, the psychotic state that sometimes follows withdrawal from alcohol, which is a dream depressant, after prolonged drinking. In delerium tremens, the hallucinations appear to be the breakthrough of the suppressed REM state into consciousness, and the sleep of the alcoholic in such a state is found to consist almost 100% of REM sleeping. All of this indicates that dreaming is essential for health.

Earlier experimenters in sleep and dreaming invented various hypotheses to explain why REM sleep was so important. Fortunately, scientific explanations of the importance of dreams and REM sleep are available from depth psychology. At the turn of the century Sigmund Freud, C. G. Jung, and their colleagues, began a psychological exploration of the meaning and function of dreams that has proved enormously fruitful. Freud was the first to publish a psychological theory of dreams in his ground-breaking book, *The Interpretation of Dreams*. The book was hardly a best seller. The first edition consisted of only six hundred copies and it took eight years to sell them.[6] This attests to the resistance of the lay and professional public to its revolutionary ideas, not to the quality of the book.

Freud's dream theory was rooted in his theory of man: i.e., the fundamental energy in man is sexual libido, which always strives for pleasure and gratification. In the way, however, is the Super Ego, the moral standpoint in the human being, which denies the gratification of the instinctual energies, and, since the Super Ego operates unconsciously, represses them. As a result a disturbance is set up in which the instinctual energies seek their gratification, and the repressing mechanisms try to keep them submerged. Dreams, Freud felt, reflect this situation. Primarily they express forbidden wishes of the instinctual energies in man. Since these wishes are forbidden they do not appear directly in dreams but are disguised. So, for Freud, dreams had a latent and manifest dream content. The manifest dream content was what the dream *seemed* to be about; the latent content was what it was *actually* about. To understand the meaning of a dream one had to get beneath the manifest content to the underlying latent content.

Freud's great contribution came because he was able to see, and scientifically establish, the independence of psychological processes. Human ills, he saw, could be produced, and cured, by purely psychic means. However, in his biologically oriented theory of man, Freud was not able to transcend the materialistic standpoint of his day. Man remained, for Freud, a material being, and his energies were purely biological. This so dominated Freud's thinking that his theory of dreams was made to submit to his basic assumptions. With his idea that a dream had a manifest content and a latent one he could, of course, bend any dream to fit his theory. Like the robber of Greek mythology, Procrustes, who waylaid travellers and made them fit his bed by shortening them or stretching them, so Freud could make any dream fit his theory.

---

[6]*The Life and Work of Sigmund Freud* by Ernest Jones, edited and abridged by Lionel Trilling and Steven Marcus; Basic Books, Inc., New York, 1961, p. 234.

Jung objected to Freud's insistence that man's psychic energy was exclusively sexual and biological. He was free of Freud's materialistic bias, and could not accept Freud's idea that dreams concealed their true meaning beneath a facade. Jung felt that man's energies could go in many directions— into sexuality, art, creative endeavors of all kinds, or destructive directions—but that the basic drive behind man's energy was the drive to wholeness. He saw that man had a spiritual, as well as a biological nature. He felt dreams expressed man's living reality and essence; they not only portrayed the forces within man, but also were in the service of man's higher development. Jung specifically rejected Freud's theory of a manifest and latent dream content. The dream, said Jung, means exactly what it says. Nature does not lie, and the dreams do not lie. In favor of Jung's rejection of the theory of a disguised latent dream content is the fact that dreams seem to bring up the most outlandish things. Far from disguising morally objectionable things about ourselves, they often confront us with the most embarrassing symbols. If we do not readily understand what the dreams are saying, Jung pointed out, it is not because their real meaning is disguised under a facade, but because dreams speak a symbolic language that we do not understand. To be scientific about dreams, Jung urged, we must not impose upon them a theory into which they are compelled to fit, but must allow each dream to speak for itself. It will be our task in this book to see more deeply what this means.

Human development is like a tree that must be rooted in the earth in order to grow. The problem of our time is that we are like uprooted trees. Our roots no longer extend down into the inner depths to nourish us, so our growth cannot reach upward into the realm of the spirit. Our task will be to see how dreams are like roots that reach far down into the nourishing depths of the earth of our souls, and help energy flow upward so our growth and development are possible.

King Nebuchadnezzar's Dream

The 30th verse of the 2nd chapter of the Book of Daniel states in one sentence the essentials of Jung's theory of dreams. King Nebuchadnezzar had a dream and wanted it interpreted, for not only did he, as an ancient Babylonian, believe in dreams, but as the King he believed God might be sending him a message of importance for the safety of his throne, and the welfare of his kingdom. The problem was that he could not remember what the dream was.

Not being able to recall dreams is a problem that many people share with King Nebuchadnezzar. As we have seen, laboratory research on sleep and dreaming shows that all of us spend about an hour and a half each night in dream sleep, but some people say they are not able to recall their dreams. Usually we can train ourselves to remember our dreams by keeping a pad and pencil by the bed and, immediately upon awakening, looking within to see if a dream image is floating through our minds. Whatever we recall should be written down, even if it seems fragmentary, for sometimes if we write down the fragment the whole dream will come back.

Sometimes people say they do not remember their dreams, when they do in fact have some dream recall, but have ignored their dreams because something seemed to say to them that what they remembered was not important. It is as though a voice declared, "Don't bother writing that down; it is only a rehash of what went on at the office." Or, "Ignore that, it is only a meaningless fragment." We must pay no attention to such disparaging thoughts, which merely reflect the collective opinion of our times that wants to discourage such things as dreams. It is important to record whatever comes to us, no matter how insignificant it may seem to be at the time, for the discipline of writing down what we remember encourages deeper and more complete dream recall in the future. Besides, it is often surprising what meaning there is in seemingly "insignificant" dreams. I have often found when people say, "Oh yes, I had a dream, but I am sure it means nothing," that it is precisely *this* dream that contains an important message.

Remembering dreams can be likened to fishing. The fisherman stands by the side of the water with the faith that there *are* fish out there even though he cannot see them. By patience, diligence, sensitivity, and intuition he may catch a fish and bring it up from the depths of the water. Dreams, like fish, may be caught by us and lifted up from the depths of the unconscious into the light of awareness. The difference is that the fish of the unconscious, those living contents that emerge in our dreams, often act as though they *want* to be caught. They attach themselves to our line, so to speak, and seek the light of day. However, we must take the trouble to put the line out and bait it with our expectancy.

Dream recall is also aided by certain things, and disturbed by others. If we are too busy in the outer world, if we are bombarded by radio or TV, or constantly involved in extraverted activities or concerns, dream recall will suffer. It has also been shown that alcohol greatly inhibits dream recall, as do most drugs and sedatives. On the other hand, a time of quiet reflection before going to sleep at night or, better yet, a whole day of introversion, will help our ability to remember our dreams. You can't catch fish if you startle them by blundering around making a lot of noise, and so it is with the contents of the unconscious.

The religions of the world have always known this. Bishop Synesius of the early Christian Church, for instance, recommended that people who desire dreams should pray for them. Elijah, in need of communion with God, journeyed alone far out into the wilderness to the cave on Mt. Sinai and there talked with Him. Jesus retired to the solitude of the desert to pray. The American Indian searched for a guiding dream by undertaking a solitary Vision Quest with a pilgrimage to a sacred spot in the mountains or hills. The supplicant who came to the Temple of Asklepius, Greek god of healing, to seek healing from the god in a dream, slept in a special chamber of the temple in a state of solitary incubation.

In spite of everything, however, some people say they do not remember dreams. Undoubtedly dream recall varies from one person to another. Some people have the kind of personality that allows in contents of the unconscious readily, and others have, as it were, a stronger, thicker wall around the ego that screens things out. William James spoke of the "tough-minded-hunters" and the "tender-minded visionaries." Introverted, intuitive people are usually more likely to remember dreams than extraverted people who are more oriented to the realities of the outer world than the images of the inner world. There is no psychological or spiritual virtue in simply remembering dreams. It is what we do with our dreams and our lives that is important.

King Nebuchadnezzar could not remember his dream, but that did not stop him from asking the wise men of his court to interpret it for him. "Tell your servants the dream, and we will reveal its meaning for you,"[7] they said to him. The position of the dream interpreters seems reasonable, for how could they interpret the dream without knowing what it was? But Nebuchadnezzar was not a reasonable man, and demanded that they give him both the dream and its meaning. If not, he said, he would have them all executed.

So the order was given that all the dream interpreters of the land were to be killed. This included the Hebrew prophet Daniel, and his three friends, Hananiah, Mishael, and Azariah, for they, too, were wise men of the court. To save his life and that of his friends, Daniel went into a trance, and in his trance the dream was revealed to him. Daniel then presented himself to Nebuchadnezzar who asked him to tell him his dream, and why it had come to him. Daniel answered, "This mystery has been revealed to me . . . for this sole purpose: that the king should learn what

---

[7]Daniel 2:4

it means, and that you should understand your inmost thoughts."[8]

In this one sentence Daniel has said a great deal. We can begin with his reference to "inmost thoughts." This is translated in various ways. For example, the Revised Standard Version says " . . . that you may know the thoughts of your mind." The King James version says "that thou mightest know the thoughts of thy heart." In the Bible the heart is generally a synonym for what we would call today the unconscious. The best way to put it would be that Daniel is saying that the dream comes from a secret mind within Nebuchadnezzar, from an inmost mind that is different from his conscious mind. This inmost mind is like an inner world, a vast part of ourselves that is psychic, but not identical with consciousness and so has been called the unconscious.

Jung spoke of the "unconscious" mind because it is something of which we are ordinarily unaware. What the unconscious mind actually is we do not know, but we do know its manifestations in dreams, visions, patterns of behaviour, affects, myths, fairy tales, and neuroses. Like the atom, which cannot be observed directly but whose nature can be deduced from its effects, so the unconscious mind cannot be observed directly, but can be studied through what it produces in our field of consciousness. It is from this inmost mind, Daniel says, that is, from the unconscious, that the dreams come.

Freud, as we have seen, formulated a theory of the unconscious mind and was the first to present scientific evidence of its existence. For Freud the unconscious consisted of personal memories that have been forgotten or repressed, or certain instinctual urges that have been banished from consciousness due to their morally disturbing nature. Jung agreed with Freud that there was this realm of the "personal" unconscious, but went much further and declared that there was also the realm of the "collective unconscious" (which he later called the "objective psyche"). The personal

---

[8]Daniel 2:30

unconscious is made up of elements from our own personal
life story, but the collective unconscious contains patterns
for life, and living symbols and images, that are part of our
basic, given psychic nature and do not come from personal
life experience.

To speak of the collective unconscious is to say that
human beings have a certain common psychic structure.
Just as we all have a common physical structure, so we all
have a common psychic structure. No one doubts for a moment, for instance, the universal nature of the human body.
We all have a heart, lungs, kidneys, an immunization system, etc., and these all function in the same way in each of
us. This is why a doctor can treat any human being because
the human body has a common denominator and functions
in much the same way whether the doctor is treating an
Australian aborigine or a cultivated Englishman. It is the
same with the psyche, which also has a common structure,
and a universal way of functioning.

The common elements in the human psyche that cor-
respond to the common elements in the human body, such
as the heart, lungs, kidneys, Jung called the *archetypes*. Archetypes are the basic building blocks of the personality.
They are patterns of energy which, when released, shape
consciousness, and influence the development and expression of our personality in definite ways. The archetypes are
inherited patterns that express themselves in human behaviour, emotions, fantasies, and ideas. They are unlearned
patterns of life, analogous to the unlearned patterns of life
that are found, for instance, in insects, migrating birds, and,
indeed, in all forms of animal and plant life.

The archetypes are the psychological representations of
the instincts, but whereas we think of an instinct in terms of
its physical expression, an archetype includes not only the
physical side but also a pattern of imagery, emotion, and
meaning. When an archetype is activated it impels us to a
certain physical activity, but accompanying this are images
and fantasies in our minds, and characteristic emotions. If
we could see into the depths of the archetype, we would also
perceive there its meaning. Out of this comes an instinctive

sense of direction for our lives and our consciousness.

An example would be the experience of "falling in love." To fall in love is a typical human experience, showing that it has an archetypal basis. When this occurs we feel a sexual urge, our consciousness is flooded with fantasies of the beloved, we experience a release of profound emotions, and, at the heart of it, there is a deep meaning. We experience this state as a unique one. Of course it is entirely unique to us, but the language of love is astonishingly the same all over the world. What is unique is that the experience has come to us, certain human beings, but the experience as such is as old as human life, that is, it is archetypal.

The collective unconscious is the sum total of the archetypes. It is the basic substratum of our psychic life. It seems to contain the stored up wisdom of many millions of years as life has evolved over the millenia. So it has an impact upon us that is profound, and often brings to us a great wisdom, for to realize the collective unconscious is to come into contact with a source of wisdom far beyond ourselves, the wisdom of life itself.

It is no more unusual to believe in the universality of the psyche than it is to speak of the universality of the human body. Of course, at the same time human life is also unique. All human bodies have the same structure, yet no two are exactly alike. So with our personalities. Your particular personality has never existed before. There is something unique about you, something that is just you. As long as we live life unconsciously we tend to be like everyone else. Then the archetypes mould us into unconscious functioning patterns, they shape us into the same mould as they shape mankind in general, and we become collective man. But if we adopt our own particular conscious attitude to the unconscious, if we become aware of what we are, and the unique element that is in us, an individual development takes place. The same archetypes which, when we were living unconsciously moulded us into a kind of common man, help us become individuals when we relate to them in a conscious way.

So the collective unconscious not only contains the wisdom of the past, it also contains the energy for the future. Life constantly strives to bring about unique and new forms. In the very heart of the unconscious lies the deep instinct to bring about a whole, unique personality in us. Jung called this the urge to individuation, that is, to become an undivided person, whose conscious personality is at one with the unconscious. He saw the urge to individuation as the fundamental instinct in life, as the religious instinct in man that impels him to seek the wholeness and completion that seems to be God's intention for man. No one, of course, ever becomes completely individuated or whole. There are always too many new possibilities in us for this to be realized in our lifetime. It is the process that is important, and it is this process of becoming a more developed person that gives life its interest and meaning.

The evidence for the existence of the personal unconscious, the collective unconscious, and the archetypes, has been amply presented in many places by Jung and his colleagues, and to try to repeat or summarize it would take us too far afield from our subject. Suffice it to say that when Daniel speaks of the "inmost thoughts," there is a reality behind his words. There *is* an inmost mind, and it is from this realm that the dream emerges.

Dreams can be said to express the thoughts of the unconscious, but these thoughts are not like those of consciousness. Consciousness thinks in words, employs logical analysis, and utilizes concepts and ideas. The unconscious thinks primarily in symbols, images, and stories that are very much like parables.

We speak of "symbolic thinking" when something known and familiar is used to express something unknown and unfamiliar. Psychic reality is not perceived directly or through the senses of the body, but is only seen through the eye of the soul. The psychic world is ordinarily invisible to us, but it *is* represented in the images of our dreams. We may dream of houses, animals, trees, mountains, fantastic creatures, or other human beings. These symbolize the reality of our inner life. The language of the unconscious is an "as if" language, and every dream could be preceded by the words "it is like this in your soul today." Jesus speaks in the same way in his parables, saying, "The kingdom of heaven is like a mustard seed which a man took and sowed in his field."[9] The kingdom of heaven is not a mustard seed, but is *like* a mustard seed. The mustard seed, something known and familiar, is used to symbolize the kingdom of heaven, something unknown and unfamiliar. This is the kind of symbolic thinking that we find in our dreams.

The language of the unconscious can be compared to a foreign language. If we want to learn a foreign language we will have to spend a lot of time learning its vocabulary and grammatical structure. Learning a foreign language is not a simple matter; if we are serious about it we must expect to expend a considerable amount of time and effort. In the same way, if we want to understand our dreams we will have to work hard, and must expect to become as one who is under instruction. If we want our spiritual life to be given to us in a convenient box that does not require much effort on our part, we had better not look to our dreams for help, for our dreams will place considerable demands upon us. Nevertheless, we *can* learn the language of dreams, for it is not dreams that are obscure, but our understanding of them. No one would look at something written in a foreign language he had not studied and say it was obscure; rather he would recognize that it was his lack of knowledge that made the language unintelligible to him. So with dreams. Once the language of a dream has been understood it is often a. marvel of clarity.

Daniel goes on to say that the inmost thoughts have come to Nebuchadnezzar in his dream for the sole purpose that he might understand them. So the prophet tells us that dreams come *for a purpose*. This is perhaps the most impressive single thing about dreams: the fact that there is behind them a purposive, intelligent action. It is as though they are devised by some Center within us that has a point of view and scope of understanding that goes beyond our consciousness. To truly understand the meaning of a dream is

---

[9]Matthew 13:31

to be confronted by a psychic intelligence within us that knows something we do not know and that has a purpose all its own. To see this purposeful activity unfold in a series of dreams is still more impressive. This purposive quality of dreams comes because they seem to be in the service of the individuation process of which we just spoke. As though proceeding in a spiral motion, the dreams lead us around and around an unseen inner Center that represents our wholeness and in this lies the ultimate purpose behind them.

But there must be changes in consciousness if individuation is to occur. Our conscious personality must continually grow and expand if the unconscious potentiality within us is to be realized. This is why Daniel says that the dreams come for the sole purpose that Nebuchadnezzar may *understand* his inmost thoughts. If we understand something, we have added something to ourselves. To understand something is to become more conscious. It is to add a bit of knowledge to ourselves and with this the range of our consciousness is expanded.

There are, however, two ways of arriving at understanding or knowledge. The first way can be communicated from one person to another. We can understand a technique or learn a number of facts through a process of education or through certain commonly shared experiences. This kind of knowing is public, and is open to everyone who has the necessary talent. If I wish to understand calculus I can go to school, and, provided I have the necessary mental equipment, I can learn to do calculus. Anyone else with the requisite intellectual equipment can do the same thing, and the imparting of knowledge in this way is what education is all about. But there is another kind of knowing or understanding that can only come about privately, through being revealed. Knowledge of oneself and knowledge of God come under this category. No one can give us this knowledge, nor can we learn it from books. It only comes through a kind of initiation, or personal experience. If I want to understand what it means to love, for instance, I can read all the books in the world and still not know. I must, myself, love someone; then perhaps I will begin to understand what love is.

The understanding we get through our dreams is of this sort. Each dream is a personal experience in which there is revealed to us a bit of knowledge about ourselves. It is knowledge that comes through an "aha!," an insight or illumination, that leaves us a more conscious and developed person than we were before.

Here, then, is a basic theory of dreams: they originate from another dimension of the personality which, because we are not ordinarily aware of it, we call the unconscious. The unconscious addresses us in a symbolic language; if we are to understand its "thoughts" we have to learn how to read the language. There is a purpose behind the dream, which is to enlarge our personality and increase the scope of our lives, and when we understand the meaning of our dreams, we are put in touch with this larger purpose that is at work within us. The fact that the prophet Daniel could say all this so succinctly some 2100 – 2600 years ago[10] suggests that the knowledge of dreams is very ancient and has belonged to wise men and women for many centuries. It is only in recent times that this wisdom has been forgotten.

The Different Levels of Dreaming

When we record our dreams it soon becomes evident that they differ in quality and intensity. There are, for instance, what might be called ordinary dreams, and there are the "big dreams" that so impressed primitive people. Or, if we prefer the descriptive analysis of the early Christian philosopher, Tertullian, there are dreams which are due to the natural functioning of the soul, while others are sent by God.[11]

Many of our dreams are what I call "daily housecleaning" dreams. These are the dreams that reflect and comment upon the events of our daily lives. They may sort out the events that transpired the day before, or prepare us for the

---

[10]The dating of the Book of Daniel is uncertain. Scholars generally place it between the 2nd and 7th centuries B.C.

[11]Tertullian, "*Treatise On The Soul*," chs. XLVI-XLIX.

day to come. No single one of these dreams may seem of crucial importance, but taken as a whole such dreams are extremely helpful in keeping our minds clear and our inner house in order.

Paying attention to such dreams may be likened to brushing our teeth. If we fail to brush our teeth for a night or two there is no great problem, but if we neglect to brush our teeth for several months, we are in for an expensive trip to the dentist. So with our daily housecleaning dreams. We can, perhaps, afford to neglect our inner lives for a short time, but if we neglect the flow of our daily lives too long, we become ill. These ordinary dreams come to help us live our lives as consciously as possible, and to remain, so to speak, "on center" even in the midst of the confusion and struggles of daily existence.

To understand such dreams it is necessary to be familiar with the everyday circumstances that surround them. We need to reflect upon what is happening in our lives at the time, what kind of circumstances we find ourselves in, what transpired the day before or what is facing us tomorrow. An older middle-aged woman dreamt that she was in bed with a particularly disagreeable man whom she knew and did not trust. The dream continued:

"I thought, I wonder if he thinks he's going to make it with me. I believe I was looking for the bathroom when all of a sudden there were other Alcoholics Anonymous members in the room too. 'This isn't my place,' I said, 'how did I get here?' I asked a woman. She whispered to me, 'Maybe you were drinking.' I said, 'Oh no! Now I won't be able to receive my 25th birthday cake!' I thought, 'I won't say anything; I'll get it anyway.' Then I thought, 'But they will know.' I awoke, relieved it was a dream."

To understand this dream we need to know that this woman is a recovered alcoholic, and as a member of Alcoholics Anonymous she is devoted to the program that helps her keep from drinking. We also need to know that it is the custom in her Alcoholics Anonymous group for a person to receive a birthday cake after each year of completed sobriety. We need to know, too, that when she was drinking many years ago she was involved in a great deal of self-deception, and that to remain sober she must be absolutely honest with herself.

But the final key to understanding the dream came from an incident a few days before in which she had borrowed a tape from her church library and in the process of making a copy she had somehow erased the original. "I had some misgivings," she said, "because I wanted to borrow another tape and if I told them what happened they might not let me, so I turned it (the now ruined original tape) in and said nothing. The following week I thought the tape lady looked at me suspiciously."

Clearly, our dreamer has a guilty conscience because she did not tell the people at her church that she had erased the tape, and her dream brings up the disagreeable matter after she had decided to cover it up. Any kind of self-deception is, for this woman, going back to her previous alcoholic psychology. The man she does not trust can be understood as a personification of the voice in her that counseled her not to say anything about the tape lest she not be allowed to have any more. The woman who whispers to her, "Maybe you were drinking" refers to her previous deviousness, which she has heroically overcome with the help of Alcoholics Anonymous, but which now endangers her again.

It was not difficult for this woman to see the meaning of her dream, but then she had to act upon it, which is often the way it is with dreams. So she called the church and told the woman in charge of the tapes what she had done. As one might have suspected, it was not a grave matter and the affair ended nicely. But if she had not done this it would have gone badly with her. She simply had to keep her inner house in order, and the dream came for that purpose. The seriousness of the situation was reflected in the fact that when she woke up she "was glad it was *only a dream*"—

always a sure indicator that a matter of great urgency is being brought up.

There are other dreams, however, that do not yield their meaning even when we take into account what is going on in our daily lives. To understand these dreams we may have to reflect upon our life history. We may need to recall things from our childhood, our relationship to our parents, or the history behind some previous marriage. At this point the psychologist who is working with such dreams will need some biographical history as these dreams reach further back into the life of a person. It is as though they are seeking to heal an old wound, relieve the soul of the effects of a previous traumatic experience, or help a person make sense of his life by integrating his personal past through remembering and understanding it.

A middle-aged man dreamt of a beautiful Italian courtyard with a statue of Christ in the center. I was tempted to launch immediately into a discussion of the archetypal symbolism of courtyards, and the meaning of Christ as a psychological symbol of wholeness, but stopped to ask the dreamer what he thought about in connection with this scene. He responded at once: this was the very place in Italy where, as a young soldier in the American Army in World War II, he had killed his first German. He had been in this courtyard when a young German had come around the corner. Both had raised their rifles at the same time but he had fired first and the German fell. He never forgot the look on the German boy's face as the bullet hit and he had his last instant of life. The dreamer was a peace-loving man, and this, and other experiences in the war, had upset him greatly. So we discussed his war experiences at length. It was as though his dream had brought them up in order that they might be shared and their traumatic effects healed.

Then there are dreams that are especially charged with psychic energy. These are "numinous" dreams. The word numinous comes from the Latin word *numen* which means a presiding spirit or deity. We experience something as numinous if it partakes of the nature of an autonomous spir-

itual reality that exists beyond our personal nature. It is of
the nature of archetypes that they have a numinous quality.
Professor Rudolph Otto has shown[12] that this is the chief
characteristic of God in the Bible: His Holiness consists of
His numinosity. In the presence of the Holy God of Israel,
Otto points out, the human being experiences feelings of
dread, wonder, awe, and creatureliness. Numinosity is the
stuff of religious experience.

Numinous dreams emerge from the collective unconscious. Their numinosity comes from the archetypes, for
archetypes are numinous. They transcend the personal life
experience of the individual and so affect us more deeply.
Archetypal dreams can often be recognized because they are
not made up of the ordinary "life stuff" of our daily lives. If
we dream of freeways, of home or office, of familiar people,
that is one thing. If we dream of men from outer space,
strange animals, snakes, larger-than-life human figures, a
magical creature such as a flying horse, or a baby so precoc-
ious it begins to talk as soon as it is born, we are in the realm
of the collective unconscious. Such dreams may come at
crises in life, or point the way to a major new personality
development that must be attained, or they may come to
persons who are deeply involved in their individuation process.

The symbols in dreams of this kind may be totally unfamiliar to the dreamer, but can often be shown to have
parallels in mythology, fairy tales, and religious symbolism.
To understand such dreams it is extremely helpful to have a
wide knowledge of such subjects. The more we know about
mythology and comparative religion, poetry and literature,
the more we are able to recognize and understand archetypal dreams. This is why an analyst who is trained in
the Jungian tradition is expected to immerse himself in the
lore of man's archaic past, and why a narrowly scientific
training does not equip a person to deal with the symbolism
of dreams.

It is impossible in this brief introduction to cite all the

---

[12]Rudolph Otto, *The Idea of the Holy*; Oxford University Press, 1950.

evidence of the existence of archetypal symbols and motifs in dreams; the interested reader must pursue the extensive literature on this subject for himself. An example, however, will illustrate what it means to speak of archetypal dreams. It is taken from the book, "*The Children of Sanchez*," in which a sociologist, Oscar Lewis, interviews the four children of a poor Mexican, Sanchez, who lives in Mexico City, and reports his interviews verbatim (translated, of course, into English).

One of the children, Consuelo, occasionally reported dreams, although she never offered interpretations. The particularly vivid dream, which is our example, occurred at a time of desperate crisis in the life of the whole family. The mother had died. The children fought bitterly, and there was such hostility between Consuelo and one of her brothers that Consuelo was afraid he would try to kill her if he got the chance. "Once he tried to strangle me," she related, "banging my head against the headboard of the bed." She felt such horror toward her home that she was afraid to come home, but she had nowhere else to go. The father alternately loved and hated the children, and fluctuated between affection and brutality in his treatment of them. Nevertheless, the father seemed to provide the only potential in the family for improvement, although that potential was not being fulfilled. All of this psychological stress was aggravated by extreme poverty. At the time of the dream Consuelo was a young girl of about eleven. She dreamed as follows:

"My father had moved the bed and the shelf of the saints to a different wall. Manuel and Roberto (her brothers) were in the bedroom, Maria (her sister) and I in the kitchen. One of the panels of the bedroom door was only half-closed and I looked in. I saw my father leaning over the bed, holding in his hands a heart, the heart he had torn from the body of a young painter, Oton, who lived in the same tenement. Oton was lying on the bed, face upward. I could see the cavity from which his heart had been torn. My father was holding the heart high and offering it to somebody. I had a terrible fright and awoke with the same cry that I always make when I dream. I have never been able to get rid of that sight of my father holding that bloody heart in his hands.[13]

Consuelo made no comment on her dream, but since we know a lot about her situation at the time, we can hazard an interpretation. Many elements of the dream are quite familiar: her father is there, her brothers and sister, and the young painter, Oton. It is also set in her own home and the Christian saints are figurines in the household. What is extraordinary is the action of her father, who engages in a violent ritualistic sacrifice of the young painter. This occurs after the removal of the Christian saints from the wall. The action of the father cannot fail to remind anyone who knows Aztec mythology of the Aztec priests who sacrificed thousands of young victims each year to the sun god, Huitzilopochtli. The priests performed the sacrifices just as the father does in the dream: with a quick movement of the knife the heart of the victim would be torn out still alive and bleeding and cast as a sacrifice to the god. A piece of ancient mythology has repeated itself in this dream.

Why has this occurred? It helps to understand the meaning behind the ancient Aztec ritual. Each night the sun god, Huitzilopochtli, descends under the earth for his dangerous nightly voyage. Each dawn he must mount up again into the sky, but to do so he must defeat the demons, who are the stars. A tremendous struggle takes place at dawn and there is the ever-present danger that Huitzilopochtli's strength will not be sufficient and that the star-demons will win. That would amount to a catastrophe for mankind; in fact, such catastrophes were said to have already occurred four times in ancient days, and another such cosmic catastrophe was predicted for the future by Aztec mythology.

Huitzilopochtli's strength had to be equal to his task if

---

[13]Oscar Lewis, *The Children of Sanchez;* Vintage Books, 1966, p. 108. (Hard back published by Random House, 1961).

mankind was to survive, hence the sacrifices, for the living blood of the victims who were in the prime of life renewed the life of the god. Just as the blood of Christ is said to renew the life of the faithful worshipper, so the blood of the sacrificial victim renewed the life of the god on whom all mankind depended. The sacrifices were performed, then, for the sake of mankind, to avert a disaster, and, specifically, to enable the power of light to triumph over the powers of darkness and evil.

Psychologically, Consuelo and her family were in just such a desperate situation. The power of light in the whole family was about to be eclipsed by dark, destructive forces. Something desperate had to be done. The power of the god in the family, that is, energy of the psychic center that makes for wholeness, had to be renewed. The Christian religion of the family, it seemed, was only a veneer, ineffective against the dark forces at work, and so the saints were removed from the wall and the way was cleared for a pre-Christian mythological event to take place. The point of the dream can be understood as an attempt by the unconscious to renew the life of Consuelo, and the whole family, by renewing the positive forces and energies, and strengthening them against the destructive forces that were at work.

Did Consuelo know about this ancient Aztec mythology? Probably not. Such education as she had was from Roman Catholic sources and it was not likely that she learned of this ancient lore. Whatever knowledge she had of Aztec mythology, if any, must have been extremely perfunctory. This does not deter the dream, however, from drawing upon this ancient symbolism in order to make its point. Dreams are perfectly capable of incorporating mythological motifs and religious symbols from man's ancient past that are not part of the dreamer's conscious knowledge. No one example, such as this one, is, by itself, convincing, but when example after example is experienced, it becomes evident that there is a layer of the psyche available to the dream that far transcends our personal life experience. In the second part of this book there will be other examples of dreams from the collective unconscious that will further illustrate the archetypal role in dreams.

To suggest that dreams come from three different levels, daily life, the personal unconscious, or the collective unconscious, is a schematic representation. Actually all the layers may get mixed in together in a single dream. Nevertheless, it does help to remember that dreams may come from various layers of the psyche, and this accounts in part for their degrees of intensity and the effects they have upon us. It helps us understand why we need to reflect upon the individual circumstances of our lives in order to understand our dreams, and why, sometimes, we need to have a larger understanding of mankind's spiritual legacy as well.

There are also some dreams of a special sort. Sometimes, for instance, extrasensory perception comes through dreams. Dreams may convey to us information about events yet to come, or put us in touch with something happening to someone at a distance from us. Such dreams usually involve events of importance, or people to whom we are close. They are usually touched off by some crisis, and, if they anticipate a future event, seem to come to prepare us for some crucial, vital action. For instance, in my previous book[14] I reported a dream that came three times to a woman in which she saw her small son lying face down in the water of her swimming pool. One day, without quite knowing why, she found herself rushing to the back yard where her son was lying face down in the swimming pool. Her quick action resulted in saving the boy's life; her dreams seemed to prepare her on some level for this vital act.

Extrasensory perception dreams are rare, but they do occur. They are often troublesome to people because it is usually difficult to use the information they give. It is also sometimes difficult to know when a dream is conveying information about the future or about someone else, and only experience can tell. It is always good to keep in mind, however, that the vast majority of dreams are about us and our souls, and are not concerned with matters of clairvoyance or precognition.

---

[14]John A. Sanford, *Dreams: God's Forgotten Language*, J. B. Lippincott, 1968, p. 65.

A fascinating area about which too little is known relates to dreams and the diagnosis and treatment of physical illness. The attempt to diagnose physical illness through dreams is ancient. The Greek physician, Galen, for instance, used this method, and so did the shamans of primitive cultures. A scientific approach to diagnosing illness through dreams has not yet been worked out, but there is no doubt that there are dreams that comment upon our physical condition, especially when an illness is impending that has not yet been recognized. C. G. Jung gave several examples of dreams that commented upon physical illness,[15] and showed that the dreams represented the body through appropriate symbols. A horse, for instance, may be used by a dream to represent the animal life energy of the body, or a house to express the idea of the body as the dwelling place of the soul.

One man who complained of a chronic loss of energy in the late mornings and afternoons had a dream of a hydroelectric generating plant that spewed out vast amounts of energy in a short time and then stopped. The hydroelectric generating plant can be taken as a symbol for the body, for the body also generates a great amount of energy. If this is so, the dream seems to be saying that there is something wrong with the dreamer's body; it produces its energy chaotically, spilling it out early in the day, and then producing nothing. An examination of the dreamer's way of life showed that he was not eating properly. He had a light breakfast, too many refined sugars, and an inadequate lunch. The high sugar diet caused his body to disgorge energy quickly, but the inadequate nutrition kept his body from maintaining a steady flow. His doctor also found a liver condition that was cured by reducing alcohol intake to zero. With better nutrition, no alcohol, and better exercise his physical functions returned to normal, but if he had not dealt with his body correctly he could have become permanently ill. His dream seemed to be a warning.

Just as dreams may refer to our physical health, so they

---

[15] cf. C. G. Jung, CW Vol. 18, *The Symbolic Life*, pp 65-66 and *Letters, Vol. II*, p. 58.

also sometimes speak of impending death. A startling example came to my own father, and has been recorded in my previous book *Dreams: God's Forgotten Language*.[16] Death is not ordinarily shown in dreams by the death of the dreamer. If we have a dream in which we die it usually portends the need for a great psychological change, for all change requires the death of something in order that something new may develop. The death of the body is another matter, which might be symbolized in dreams in many ways, for instance, by the dying of a horse (representing the death of our physical energy), or by a ship breaking up at sea (representing the dissolution of the Self that carries us through life).

My father's dream came to him after an illness of some eight years. He was not a man who paid attention to his dreams, but this one made such a profound impression upon him that he related it to my mother, who wrote it down. Both of them recognized that the dream was a portent of death, which, in fact, came a week later when he died peacefully sitting in a chair one evening.

"In the dream he awakened in the living room. But then the room changed and he was back in his room in the old house in Vermont as a child. Again the room changed to Connecticut (where he had his first job), to China, to Pennsylvania (where he often visited), to New Jersey, and then back to the living room. In each scene after China, I (my mother) was present, in each instance being of a different age in accordance with the time represented. Finally he sees himself lying on the couch back in the living room. I am descending the stairs and the doctor is in the room. The doctor says, 'Oh, he's gone.' Then, as the others fade in the dream, he sees the clock on the mantlepiece; the hands have been moving, but now they stop; as they stop, a window opens behind the mantlepiece clock and a bright light shines through. The opening widens into a door and the light becomes a brilliant path. He walks out on the path of light and disappears."

---

[16]Op. cit. p. 59

The recapitulation of his life refers to his individuation, to everything he had become. The stopping of the clock suggests, of course, that time had ended for him, while the opening up of the path of light hints strongly at a continuance of life after death.

Dreams may also refer to relationships with other people. When we dream of a familiar person there is always a question whether the dream refers to our relationship with that person, or whether that person represents a like quality in us. Only the total context of the dream can tell us. Generally, unless there is a clear reference to our relationship with that person, we do well to consider the person as representing something in ourselves, for dreams do use familiar figures in this way. Sometimes, of course, a dream can be taken both ways: as a comment on our relationship to someone else, and as a picture of what is going on within us. Though it is a rare occurrence, it is also possible for us to dream of something in the psyche of another person, to produce, as it were, someone else's dream for him. Naturally, this would be someone with whom we would be quite close.

One last comment needs to be made and this is about children's dreams. Children dream a great deal, and often spontaneously report them. Parents can help their children with their dreams by listening to them carefully and taking them seriously. However, in my view, they usually should not be interpreted, as the young child would not be likely to understand the psychology involved and needs to grow naturally without the imposition of psychological theory.

Children's dreams often come from the collective unconscious and so contain much archetypal symbolism. They frequently occur when the child's natural development is blocked in some way. Nightmarish dreams, for instance, in which a child encounters a frightening animal such as a gorilla, may represent a conflict between the child's developing ego and his instinctuality. The child is caught between these two forces. On the one hand, he needs to develop an ego that is strong enough to control his instinctual forces and not be overcome by them. On the other hand, he dare not lose touch with his instinctuality entirely or his personality will be impoverished. Another source of dream material in the dreams of children is the family situation. The child is peculiarly open to the psychological situation of the whole family, as we saw in the case of Consuelo, and many dreams of children will only yield their meaning if the underlying psychology of the family is taken into account, as Frances Wickes has shown in her valuable book *The Inner World of Childhood*.

The Healing Power in Dreams

The images of our dreams contain a healing power. The healing in our dreams is especially evident if we are in danger of being overwhelmed by the unconscious. When repressions are giving way, and the forces of the unconscious are rising up into consciousness, great anxiety results. As long as we do not understand our psychological situation, as long as we cannot get a picture of it, we are exposed to enervating anxiety, for anxiety, as James Hillman of Zurich once aptly put it, is the fear of the return of the repressed. Or, when there is a demand from within for a total reorganization of the personality, we also feel the power of the unconscious. If we do not understand our situation we might indeed be "swallowed by the dragon," with the ever present threat of a psychosis or, as we retreat into more and more tightly drawn defenses, a crippling neurosis. In such circumstances the images of our dreams give us invaluable aid in presenting us with a picture of what it is that is pressing upon us. If we work with these dream images, absorbing their meaning and trying to understand them, this activity strengthens and enlightens us, and makes a connection possible between our state of consciousness and the turbulent inner forces.

One young woman, for instance, who was on the verge of being swallowed up by tremendously tumultuous inner forces, presented a dream that said that now that she was seeing the analyst she could eat the great ball of fire "bit by bit." This is the way dreams operate. They break up the tremendous inner forces of the Self bit by bit and enable us to integrate the unconscious gradually so that we are not overwhelmed by it. The effect of this, providing we adopt the correct attitude, is the enlargement of consciousness, and the expansion of our personality.

The unconscious can be either a poison or a medicine, destructive or healing. When the unconscious is affecting us, and we do not have a picture of what is acting on us, its effects are negative. But when we have an image of what is happening within us, this same power of the unconscious is healing and transformative. This ambivalent nature of the unconscious is often symbolized in our dreams in the image of the snake or serpent. The serpent, especially the poisonous serpent, represents the paradoxical nature of the collective unconscious. To be bitten by the serpent means that we become vulnerable to the unconscious. Its "bite" can either be a destructive poison eating away at us and filling us with all sorts of strange ideas, or it can become a medicine that heals us. For this reason, the serpent, one of the most feared of nature's creatures, is in the lore of mythology the symbol for healing, transformation, and eternal life. We find this, for instance, in the healing cult of Asklepius, in which the god of healing carries a staff with a serpent entwined around it (the symbol for the medical profession today), and in the Babylonian myth of Gilgamesh in which a serpent devours the plant of immortality.

Dreams also help us by showing us what it is upon which we should focus our attention. It is easy to be overwhelmed by our fears, the confusion of life, and the myriad small and great worries that beset us. A dream gives us an image of what it is we most need to ponder. In this way dreams can lift us beyond the narrow confines of our ordinary conscious life, and present us with a larger picture. Sometimes it is surprising how the unconscious offers us through dreams an entirely different picture of ourselves than our conscious picture. We may be absorbed consciously in a variety of worries, only to find the dreams presenting us with surprisingly different images. In practice, if we contemplate the dream images we find that they have the effect of shifting us to another center and giving us a standpoint of strength from which we can do battle with the fears and conflicts of our lives.

Of course our dreams are often frightening. We may see dark things in our dreams, aspects of ourselves we wish were not there, or we may be confronted with what appears to be a truly evil power or force. The way to self-knowledge is not necessarily pleasant, and often entails the painful realization that we carry within us dangerous forces. For this reason many people prefer to have nothing to do with the unconscious; they would rather solve their problems in an outer way that does not require so much of them and allows them to remain ignorant of themselves. Dreams, however, are not in themselves evil. They may show us evil or dark forces that are threatening to us, but this is helpful, for evil is never so dangerous as when we are unaware of it. For if something within us is threatening us, it is better to know about it than to be taken over unaware.

The dream provides this helpful picture of what is going on in ourselves. To be sure, we then have to carry the tension of becoming conscious. Naturally we often resent this and wish that life were easier and simpler for us, but no one goes through life without paying a price somewhere. Becoming conscious has its own price. It is not always easy to face ourselves and what we are, nor is it easy to carry the psychological burden of our own nature. But if we do not pay the price of living consciously, we may pay the price in some other way, such as through an accident, broken relationships, alcoholism, drugs, boredom, or a physical illness. There is, for instance, the curious fact that acutely psychotic people almost never develop cancer. It is as though the psyche, being spewed out in the psychosis, does not become lodged in the body. On the other hand, many physical illnesses may develop when the psyche has been tightly controlled or contained and cannot find any kind of expression. The way between psychosis on the one hand, and a physical illness on the other hand, is to live with an awareness of the nature of our own psyche and the inner forces that make us what we are.

So while it can be a dark experience to learn about the

unconscious through dreams, it can also be a light and positive experience. Facing the dangerous, devouring side of the unconscious can be frightening, but it is also the hero's task that can lead to the winning of the great treasure. No one ever won life's great treasures without risking himself in a hero struggle with life's dark and dangerous side. Some people are called upon by life to face its dangers in outer conflicts and struggles, and some are called upon to face its dangers from within.

I have often observed, for instance, that people who are wealthy, and have no reason to suffer from any material want or need, can develop the most extraordinary psychological problems. It is as though the unconscious, in order to force development upon them and get the most out of them, creates a difficult inner situation to compensate for the outer, material well-being and security.

No one goes through life, however, without being approached by a dragon somewhere. Jung once wrote, "In myths the hero is the one who conquers the dragon, not the one who is devoured by it. . . . Also, he is no hero who never met the dragon, or who, if he once saw it, declared afterwards that he saw nothing. . . . Only one who has risked the fight with the dragon and is not overcome by it wins the hoard, the 'treasure hard to attain.'"[17]

Dreams also are healing because they provide us with energy. Sometimes the difficulty is not that we are in danger of being overwhelmed by the unconscious, but that we lack enough contact with the unconscious. Then we experience a loss of energy, and lose our sense of meaning. A depression may result, or boredom, or a nihilistic attitude. It is as though we are stranded on a desert island, or at the bottom of a dark pit from which we cannot escape.

Here the same images of our dreams can help us, for these images are charged with energy. The unconscious is an enormous energy system. There is much more psychic energy in us than we realize, and the images of our dreams

---

[17]C. G. Jung, *Mysterium Coniunctionis*, CW Vol. 14; Princeton University Press, 1963; p. 531.

have the capacity to convey this energy to us. A habit of recording and paying attention to our dreams can energize our conscious life, for dreams can transfer energy from the unconscious to consciousness. This renewal of energy from the unconscious via dreams only comes to us, of course, if we put our conscious energy into the process. If we are not willing to invest our attention, efforts, and energies in the unconscious, we will not receive a flow of energy back. For energy is a flow, it is not static. Energy must flow from consciousness to the unconscious, from the unconscious to consciousness. If it stops at any one point, the flow stops entirely.

The dream also heals because of its compensatory quality. In developing our conscious personalities we have taken only a portion of our psychic potentiality and made it our own. The larger portion of the personality has been left behind. This leaves us one-sided, and when there is added to this the natural tendency of the ego toward psychological blindness and shortsightedness, and that profound streak of egocentricity that the theologian calls original sin, it can be seen that we are all incomplete persons in need of wholeness. The dreams bring up the other point of view within us. The truths and realities that they express come from the other side of consciousness, and have the effect, when they are given proper attention and we are willing to shift our point of view, of complementing our consciousness in such a way as to bring us closer to our psychic Center. It is because of the helpfulness of this compensatory function of the dream that James Kirsch, M.D., of Los Angeles, once remarked, "The dream is always true and correct. If we could invariably understand it we should be perfect beings."[18]

To follow dreams, therefore, is much like establishing a connection between the ego and the center of the personality. This has been called the "ego-Self axis," when the Self is taken to refer to the whole or total personality, a personality that embraces the Center and the unconscious. A connection

---

[18]James Kirsch, M.D., "*The Religious Aspect of the Unconscious.*" The Guild of Pastoral Psychology, Lecture No. 1, p. 22, 1939.

between the ego and this psychic Center is of vital importance for our health and well-being. The situation may
be diagrammed as follows, and the dreams may be understood as providing the link between the smaller reality of the
ego, and the larger reality of the whole person or Self.

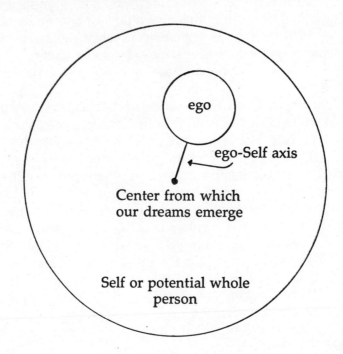

Explanation of diagram: The ego is represented by the smaller circle, and
the Self by the larger circle *and* the dot in the center, for the Self is both the
center of the personality, and also the all-embracing totality. The ego is
contained within the Self, so the smaller circle is within the larger circle.
This is true even if we are unaware of the larger personality of the Self. But
for the ego to derive the maximum benefit of a relationship with the Self
there must be the ego-Self axis, to use the term described so well by
Edward Edinger in his book *Ego and Archetype*. Dreams are one way in
which the ego-Self axis is created. Naturally, like any schematic representation, this diagram is only an approximation of the true psychological
situation.

The compensatory function of dreams accounts for the phenomenon we noted earlier, that when people are deprived of REM sleep there is a "REM Rebound" effect. We need to dream because we need the compensation that dreams bring. They hold us to our psychic Center and perform a helpful function even when we do not remember them. They are like the ballast of a ship that keeps it from capsizing in heavy seas.

But the full healing potential in our dreams will not be realized unless it is accompanied by the growth and development of consciousness. As soon as we cease to develop, the creative powers within turn negative and begin to poison us. So our dreams must be contemplated, understood when possible, and, sometimes, expressed directly in our lives by a change of direction. Consider the following dream that came to a man in his early thirties. At the time of the dream, this young man was living with his mother. After his mother came from the Midwest to take up residence with her only son in California he lost his job and became depressed. His mother was ill, and was going blind. She required a great deal of care from her son, who even had to bathe her. He was, almost needless to say a homosexual. Their relationship was one of desperate clinging on her part, and intense hatred on his part, but he refused to leave her and the hatred only came out in bursts of anger and fits of depression. He was not amenable to psychotherapy or to help of any kind, seeming to relish the miserable state of affairs in which he found himself, but he did on one occasion report a dream, which was as follows:

"My mother and I are both together in a large cup or container of water or quicksand. We are sinking. Helping arms reach out over the sides of the cup. But we don't grasp them. We hold each other and try to help each other. We both sink and are already up to our chins."

The dream gives a graphic image of the psychological situation in which he and his mother find themselves. They are like two people who are drowning, and neither one frees himself from the deadly grasp of the other to try to strike out for the safety of the shore. The dream suggests that there is hope: helping arms reach out, which may symbolize the helpful side of the dreamer's unconscious, and also outside people who are willing to help. But the help is refused. In fact, not too many months after this dream the mother died, and, shortly after that, the son became extremely depressed, tried to commit suicide, and wound up as a permanent resident in a psychiatric hospital.

The dream offered help, and tried to show this man his plight. From the point of view of the dream what he had to do was clear: he must break away from the deadly embrace of his mother, turn his back on his own regressive tendencies that held him to her, and strike out on his own. But somehow it was not in him to do this; the necessary ingredients of will and faith were lacking.

So our dreams offer us help, guidance, illumination, but do not replace that certain moral or positive attitude that we must find in ourselves if healing is to be found. Healing is a cooperative venture between the conscious personality and the unconscious. To come to the unconscious as a supplicant desiring wholeness puts us in the right attitude to find inner healing. Then we can find the help from within that comes from recalling dreams, seeking to understand them, and relating to their potential for wholeness.

The Drama and Structure of Dreams

It is said that everyone could write one novel—his own life story. From the point of view of dreams this is certainly true. A life that appears on the outside to be an innocuous, ordinary affair is seen, when viewed from the inside perspective of dreams, to be startlingly dramatic. Our dreams portray our lives as important, profound events as though our souls were a great stage on which the purpose of life either succeeds or fails. It is as though each one of us is a unique experiment, and as though we are under constant observation from within to see if the experiment taking place within us is a success or a failure. Our dreams teach us what our own life-experiment is all about, what it means to live at this particular time in history, and about our ultimate origin and destination. As we noted before, to live with dreams is to live as a person who is under instruction. Sometimes our dreams symbolize this very directly. We may dream, for instance, of going to a theater to watch a play, that is, to see our own inner drama unfold, or we may dream of being in a university where a test is to be given which we may, or may not, be prepared to take.

Our dreams are like stories, and usually we are in the dream-story, a participant in the drama. In some instances, however, we are not directly involved but simply observe the dream. In such cases it may be that the events of the dream are not yet directly affecting us, or that we are not closely enough involved in the events of our inner life, but have too detached an attitude. In those dreams in which we are involved in the action of the dream we speak of the dream ego. The dream ego is the dreamer himself, and it is clear that there is a certain correspondence between this dream ego and our waking ego, for what happens to us in our dreams is also reflected in our waking life. So if we dream that we are driving along in our car and have a flat tire we will not be surprised if the next day we feel somewhat "flat" and out of energy. Everyday language refers to this by saying that on certain days we "got up on the wrong side of bed." However, there is also a mysterious difference between the dream ego and the waking ego, for sometimes in our dreams we seem to be in possession of knowledge or information that escapes us upon awakening. This dream ego is a very important part of the dream. As we will see later on, the attitudes and decisions we make in our dreams are of crucial importance.

But the ego is only one among many dream figures. Our dreams are filled with people known and unknown, animals, monsters, and objects. We can call these various inner figures the *dramatis personae* of our dreams, and, with the exceptions noted earlier, they can be taken as personifications of partial aspects of our total personality.

Human personality is like a village of people. The early Christian philosopher Origen declared, "Understand that thou art a second little world and that the sun and moon are within thee, and also the stars." And elsewhere he wrote, "Thou seest that he who seemeth to be one is yet not one, but as many persons appear in him as he hath velleities."[19] The ego can be likened to a member of the City Council, an important personage in this village, but by no means dominant, so that the figures of our dreams are, so to speak, the villagers who make up the community of the Self.

Some of the archetypal, that is typical, figures in our dreams have become familiar to students of the psyche. There is, for instance, the shadow. The shadow is a figure who personifies those things about ourselves that do not fit into our ego ideal. The shadow includes those qualities that could belong to the ego, but do not because they are feared, or felt to be wrong. The shadow is the Mr. Hyde to our Dr. Jekyll, the despised Caliban of our souls, whom the King in Shakespeare's play *The Tempest* called, "this thing of darkness I acknowledge mine."[20] The shadow always appears in our dreams as a figure of the same sex as the dreamer, that is, as a feared, rejected or inferior woman in the dreams of a woman, and as a feared, rejected or inferior man in the dreams of a man. This is because the shadow represents attributes of the personality that *might* have been included in the development of the ego, but were rejected because they did not fit into our personal or socially conditioned image of ourselves. So, for instance, a man who was trying too hard to be good, kind, and perfect might dream of Mafia figures who represent his ruthless, amoral side. Or a woman who tries to be too controlled and spiritual might dream of a wild hussy. Experience shows, however, that fearsome though it may appear to be, the shadow personality actually contains many valuable qualities that need to be added to our conscious personality and not rejected. In the above

---

[19]Origen, *Homiliae in Leviticum*, quoted in Jung CW Vol. 16, *The Practice of Psychotherapy*, p. 197.

[20]William Shakespeare, *The Tempest*, Act V, Scene I, Line 275.

examples, for instance, the man who dreams of the Mafia figures may need to integrate into his conscious personality the masculine strength that they contain, and the woman who dreams of the wild hussy will be a more complete woman if she realizes her sexuality.

In addition, there are feminine figures in the dreams of men, and masculine figures in the dreams of women, that play vital roles in our dream life and represent very important parts of our total self. These personify the feminine qualities in a man, and the masculine qualities in a woman, for no one is all man or woman; all of us are androgynous. As men develop, they ordinarily identify their ego consciousness with their masculine qualities, and the feminine qualities fall into the unconscious and become personified as an inner woman, and vice versa with a woman. Jung has termed the feminine side of a man the *anima* and the masculine side of a woman the *animus*. These contrasexual figures greatly complicate the relationship between the sexes, and also prove crucial to our development, for only if they are accepted in the right way do we have access to the deeper layers of the unconscious.

These figures, and many others, are archetypes, because they are typical to human nature and appear in everyone. They are like essential building blocks to the psyche. The psyche develops a shadow personality along with the ego, animus or anima, just as the body will have a heart and lungs. The nature and psychology of these, and many other archetypal figures, have been discussed at length by Jung· and his colleagues, and are also dealt with in my previous books. For a more complete description of them the reader may refer to these sources.

Dreams originate from the center of the personality. It is fascinating to ponder what it is within us that devises these nightly stories that pinpoint so adroitly the needs and direction of the soul. Certainly we do not make up our dreams consciously. If we deliberately tried we would not be capable of devising such intricate, clever, and unexpected narratives as our dreams. It is as though there is a "Casting Director" within us who plans the drama, selects the actors, and directs the story. Moreover, every detail in the dream is there for a purpose, and there is always a reason why the "Casting Director" chose this particular figure rather than another.

This is not to say that dreams do not contain some admixture of consciousness. A dream is like a bit of the unconscious reaching consciousness. Consciousness, for instance, must reconstruct the dream from memory. It is always possible that in this process some of the original dream may be altered or lost; we have to trust that enough is accurately recalled. The admixture of consciousness in a dream also accounts for the fact that people occasionally say that they can wake themselves up from a dream at will, especially if their dreams become too frightening. "I told myself to wake up, and I did," is something we sometimes hear from people. It may even be possible, as is sometimes asserted, for consciousness to suggest to the unconscious what to dream about, though I strongly surmise that in such cases the unconscious uses a free hand in constructing an original dream out of the suggestion. It would be unfortunate, however, for us to consciously direct our dreams even if this could be done, for we need our dreams to give us correct and compensatory information about ourselves. It would be a great loss to us if we took away from the unconscious its autonomy in constructing our dreams. That would be a little like telling God how to advise us, or like our taking over the breathing function from the autonomic nervous system with the vain thought that we can consciously direct our breathing better than our body can.

A recent book that proposes that we try to make our dreams into what we want them to be is Patricia Garfield's book *Creative Dreaming* (Ballantine Books). In this book it is suggested that we can work in a creative way with the dream images that come to us, but it is also suggested that we try to program our dreams to be the kind of dreams we want. It is the latter process of which I am critical because, as stated above, we *need* the dream statements of the unconscious for our own health and therefore should not manipulate them. That the author is not as successful in manipulating dream images as much as she would like is suggested on page 33 where she says, "Almost all my dreams I have wanted to produce have sooner or later appeared. The induced dream does not always contain àll the elements I intended but it often does. Sometimes it contains more interesting elements as well." If the dream were analyzed, I suspect that these "more interesting elements" would contain a vital and unsuspected message that the dreamer needs to have.

One variant of programming dreams is called "lucid dreaming."[21] It calls for us to become "awake" in the dream, that is, to be able to realize in the dream that we are dreaming. This, it is said, then gives us the capacity to redirect the dream. If this capacity is used to redirect the dream in the way we would wish, that is, to give it a pleasant or pleasing ending, that would, in my view, be a great loss for the reasons I have stated. However, if such a "wakefulness" is used to give us a chance to change our reactions in the dream and select other responses, this is a different matter. Such a process would then be a form of "active imagination," a helpful process that we will discuss shortly. There is a vast difference between trying to manipulate the unconscious to suit our fancy, and altering our ego responses to what is happening, and this distinction must be kept clearly in mind.

Like a drama, a dream often has an opening scene, a development, and a conclusion. The opening scene of the dream states the problem or situation with which the dream is going to deal; it helps in understanding a dream to pay particular attention to the way the dream begins for it sets the stage for everything that is to follow. Then comes the action of the dream in which the dream develops the opening situation into a story. Generally some problem or dilemma is presented as the dream unfolds. At the conclusion

---

[21]Cf. the booklet *Lucid Dreaming, Dawning of the Clear Light* by Gregory Scott Sparrow, A.R.E. Press, Virginia Beach, 1976.

of the dream there is sometimes a solution, or hint of a solution. The Greeks called this the *lysis*. It is the unravelling of the knot, the dream's suggestion about how we can proceed toward the resolution of our difficulty. Not all dreams, however, offer us a lysis; some dreams seem to terminate in the midst of the story, as though they could not take the matter farther. Nightmares are an example. In a nightmare a tension-producing situation develops that creates more and more anxiety until suddenly we waken in fright. One reason for the nightmarish feeling is that no solution to the anxiety-producing impasse is offered by the dream. In nightmares, great tension exists between the attitude of consciousness and that of the collective unconscious. A nightmare mirrors a situation in which we are going against ourselves. Changes must take place in consciousness before the anxiety arising from the tension can be eased.

Dreams are carefully structured. Each event in a dream has its particular place in the dream. Causality, for instance, is represented in dreams by the sequence of events. In a dream, event *A* produces event *B*, which in turn produces event *C*. We ordinarily think of causality mechanistically. One billiard ball hits another and that is why the second ball moves as it does. In psychological matters, causality is a matter of inner relatedness. A particular psychological situation produces the subsequent situation. The second, as it were, grows out of, or evolves out of the first. For this reason the sequence of events in our dreams is important, for it helps us see why things develop as they do.

It is also helpful to remember that the unconscious turns toward us a reflection of the face we turn toward it. For instance, hostile figures in our dreams often represent rejected elements of our personality. If our attitude toward them changes, their face toward us changes. In my earlier book, I began with a series of dreams that illustrated this. A man had a series of dreams in which the same hostile figure repeatedly pursued him. At last, through a change in attitude in which he determined to face himself, he had a dream in which he stopped running from his pursuer, and turned to face him:

"Again," he dreamt, "I was in a warlike situation. My enemy again approached me with a knife. He wanted to kill me. I started to run, but then I stopped and, facing him, said instead, 'All right, kill me if you want to.' The enemy also stopped and paused. Then he smiled and, turning, walked away."[22]

This dream reminds us of Jesus' saying, "Agree with thine adversary quickly, whilst thou art in the way with him; lest at any time the adversary deliver thee to the judge, and the judge deliver thee to the officer, and thou be cast into prison. Verily I say unto thee, Thou shalt by no means come out thence, till thou hast paid the uttermost farthing."[23]

Similarly, a figure may appear in our dreams that is weak or deformed; it represents something in us that is not yet developed, something that, perhaps, we fear or dread, and so it has not had enough life. A retarded child may appear, representing that part of our own development that has been retarded, or an injured man or woman may represent a psychological injury within ourselves. In Stevenson's novelette *Dr. Jekyll and Mr. Hyde*, Hyde, who of course represents Jekyll's shadow personality, is described as incredibly strong and full of vital energy, but also curiously deformed in appearance. Stevenson has the lawyer Utterson say of him, "There is something wrong with his appearance; something displeasing, something downright detestable. . . . He must be deformed somewhere: he gives a strong feeling of deformity, although I couldn't specify the point."[24] Hyde's deformed appearance reflects the fact that Jekyll's shadow personality has not had much chance to live. Dreams invite us to make friends with such rejected or deformed figures and find ways in which the unlived life they contain can find suitable expression, or at least reach consciousness.

Because consciousness is so crucial in psychological de-

---

[22]*Dreams: God's Forgotten Language*, J. B. Lippincott, 1968, p. 26
[23]Matthew 5:25-26 KJV.
[24]Modern Library edition of the Selected Writings of Robert Louis Stevenson, p. 486.

velopment, the role the dream ego plays in the dream is exceedingly important. What are *you* doing in your dreams? What is your attitude toward what is happening? How do the dream figures interact with you? A dream is an experience all its own. Like any experience it tells us much about ourselves, our strengths, and weaknesses, and so throws light not only upon what is going on within the unconscious, but also upon the state of development of the ego.

A brief example will illustrate some of these points. A middle-aged woman suffering from depression had the following dream:

> "We were at home. There was a big fire burning outside. My daughter and her kitten were playing and I asked them inside as the air was poisonous. 'Do not run and dance and sing,' I said. Inside I pulled down the drapes and curtains and locked the door."

The opening scene says: "We were at home. There was a big fire burning outside."

The problem with which the dream opens is the problem of the big fire. The dreamer is not with the fire but stays safely in the shelter of her home. Fire is energy, and energy is what the dreamer lacks, so the dream seems to be speaking about her depression. The dream continues to develop its theme with the image of the young woman playing outside with the kitten. Here is a picture of more energy, of spontaneity and creative play. The kitten is a life-loving creature, and the young woman personifies naturalness and new life, and, as the dreamer's daughter, clearly has a close relationship to the conscious personality. The young woman and the kitten seem completely unafraid of the fire; evidently they are at home with it. The daughter and the kitten are the "dramatis personae" of the dream. They have been chosen by the dream because they personify helpful elements in the psyche of the dreamer that she desperately needs in order to alleviate her depression. But the dreamer interrupts their play and brings them inside with the statement that the air is poisonous.

Now "poison" represents the dangerous side of the unconscious, which the dreamer fears, but the dream is suggesting that it is the dreamer's timid attitude that is creating the fear of this poison, for there was no mention of poison in the dream until the dreamer called in the girl and the kitten. The fact is, the dreamer thinks or supposes the air is poisonous, but the dream does not say that it is poisonous (a good illustration of the importance of the details of a dream). Once the young woman and kitten are inside the house, the drapes and curtains are closed and the door is shut. Because of her fear, the dreamer shuts herself in more than ever. It is easy to see why this woman is so depressed, for all the vital energy has been left outside of the house, or taken in and suppressed. But the ending of the dream also gives a hint of a way out—a lysis: reverse the situation, open the windows, unlock the door, take a chance with that fire, and let the young woman and kitten play. The dream suggests that this woman does not need to be depressed, that with a change of attitude and a little more courage there is much potential energy and new life.

Because dreams have a certain intelligible structure, and because they so dramatically represent the inner and outer circumstances of our lives, they have proved useful to psychotherapists. The next section gives a few ideas on how psychotherapists, trained in the spirit of Jung's work with dreams, may use dream interpretation to help their clients.

The Use of Dreams in Therapy

As noted earlier, dreams have a very individual character. They are directed to an individual who is at a particular point in a life which is absolutely unique and has never been lived by anyone else before. They are like a suit of clothes that is tailor-made to fit only one person. This is one reason for their helpfulness, for dreams are an antidote to the collectiveness of human life. We are all of us products of our culture, exposed to similar influences, and subject to the same deadening effects. Collective man is strong in us, and the path of least resistance is to go through life the way everyone else is going through it.

So great is the power of collective thinking that it never occurs to us that this is the way we are. We may suppose that we are acting from free will, that we are individualistic, when, in fact, we are simply the exponent of leveling psychological forces.

It is important not to confuse the terms collective thinking and collective unconscious. In speaking of collective thinking I mean that the development, attitude, and thinking of people tends to be identical in everyone; that is, our conscious personalities are formed and conditioned by mass attitudes. The collective unconscious refers to the universal archetypal structure of the psyche that is our common human heritage. So the first term refers to the tendency to identify with the mass consciousness of our times, and the second term refers to the structure of the psyche.

There is a connection between the two, however. When we are unaware and have no insight into the archetypal forces within us, these forces tend to shape us into typical moulds and we become like everyone else. The archetypes tend to produce stereotyped forms of behavior when they possess us, that is, when we have no individual relationship to them. Then they tend to produce human beings who think and act alike all the time. However, when we develop a conscious attitude, and become aware of the unconscious forces that are within us, these same archetypal energies begin to forge a truly individual personality. It is our conscious attitude that makes the difference. To be unconsciously gripped by the archetypes is to be compelled by them to live out our lives on the most common denominator of humanity. So, for instance, the people of Nazi Germany who were swept up into the archetypes that possessed their nation during World War II exhibited a non-individual, collective human behavior. But the same archetypal forces, when faced consciously and related to by an individual consciousness, have exactly the opposite effect and begin to develop persons who are individuals.

When we are merely an exponent of collective thinking,

and miss our individuality, we always become more or less ill. The only reason we may not recognize our illness is because everyone else shares much the same symptoms. If everyone is acting the same way, no one thinks of himself as ill. For this reason, dreams are helpful in therapy, because a conscious relatedness to our dreams frees us of our unconscious identification with others and creates an individual attitude.

The first step in the practical use of dreams in therapy is to encourage a person to record his dreams. This honors the dream, fixes it in memory, and is a way of acknowledging that the ego does not have to go through life alone, but has the help of an inner partner or guide. Writing down dreams is like asking the unconscious to help us. It is also helpful in using dreams in therapy to have the client read or tell his or her dreams aloud, for in telling our dreams we re-experience them, they become more real to us, and sometimes insights into the dreams develop as we listen to the dream we are telling. Sometimes it is also helpful if the therapist repeats the dream after hearing it, partly to make sure he or she has the dream and its details correctly, and also because this enables the client to see his dream more objectively.

Now the dream is ready to be explored, and the next step is to encourage the client to associate to the dream and its various elements. What does this or that in the dream make him think of? What occurs to him about this person or that person whom the dream used in making up the dream story? This step is essential, for the meaning of the dream lies in the dreamer himself. If the therapist were to leap in too quickly with an interpretation, vital pieces of information might be missed, as we saw in the example used earlier of the man who dreamt of the courtyard in Italy.

Sometimes the dreamer comes up with associations that give the key to the dream, but sometimes one simply hears "Oh I can't think of anything in connection with that." It is a frustrating fact that the use of imagination is throttled in our culture. We are afraid to turn our minds loose and see what comes into them. Maybe we have too many memories from childhood of being ridiculed when we produced something imaginative from within ourselves, or recall humiliating experiences in the classroom. There are very few things that do not bring some associations to our mind, yet some people, dreaming of a ship for instance, may say they have no associations at all with a ship; that it doesn't make them think of anything.

When this happens I sometimes play the "Man from Mars" game. "Pretend," I say, "that I am a man from Mars. I have just come down to the planet Earth and I know nothing about it. Someone has referred to something called a 'ship' but I do not know what it is, and you have to tell me what a ship is. Explain it to me." This little game often frees the imagination of my client who gets into the game with me and explains to "the man from Mars" about ships. By the time he is through it is surprising what associations have come to him about ships, and often this opens up the meaning of the dream to the dreamer.

At other times there may be no meaningful associations to the contents of the dream because the symbolism comes from the realm of the collective unconscious. Here the knowledge of the analyst is extremely important, for the key to the meaning of our dreams, as we have seen, may be found in points of comparison between the dream and mythology, and the underlying meaning of the dream may come to light only when an examination is made of the way a particular dream symbol has been used in mythology and religious lore.

The process of association involves both client and analyst in an exploration of the dream as a living experience. It is like "walking around" in the dream, exploring it, treating it as a living experience, and discussing it just as we would relate some adventure in outer life. Robert Louis Stevenson once wrote, "There are some among us who claimed to have lived longer and more richly than their neighbours: when they lay asleep they claim they were still active; and among the treasures of memory that all men review for their amusement, these count in no second place the harvests of their dreams."[25] It helps to pursue certain questions: "How

---

[25]Robert Louis Stevenson, *Over the Plains*, "A Chapter on Dreams." p. 208; Charles Scribners Sons, Biographical Edition, 1910.

did you feel in the dream? Were you afraid? nervous? joyful?" Approaching the dream in this way we come to see that the dream belongs to us and is part of our living experience.

Care must always be taken to avoid imposing a theory upon the dream if it does not fit. Otherwise we run into the danger of making the dream fit our theory, which, as we have already seen, was the difficulty with Freud's method of interpretation. It is best to approach each dream as though we knew nothing, to let the dream develop and speak for itself, to assume at the beginning that we are ignorant of what this is all about. Only in this way can the dream properly instruct us.

Eventually an interpretation of the dream may emerge. If we have the correct interpretation, everything in the dream finds its proper place and explanation. If there are details which the interpretation does not explain, it is either because we do not understand those details or because the interpretation is incorrect or not sufficiently comprehensive. The most satisfactory dream interpretation will embrace all of the dream, and not simply dwell upon part of it, for dream interpretations are like scientific hypotheses which can be considered valid only when they include the whole range of facts under consideration. If we have an hypothesis in science which explains a number of facts, but not all of them, those unexplained details are either not seen in the correct light, or the hypothesis itself may be incomplete or in error.

We can feel most confident of a dream interpretation when it enables us to "gestalt" the dream, that is, when the interpretation gives a form to the dream as a whole. The more clearly a dream is understood the more capable we are of expressing its meaning succinctly. The less adequate the interpretation, the more likely we are to have to labor at its explanation. Often the best dream interpretations are the briefest. When the essence of the dream can be expressed in one sentence, we are most likely to be on the right track.

The question naturally arises how we can be sure when a dream interpretation is correct. Only *the dreamer* knows. When a dream has been understood correctly there is something within us that assents to it. There may be an "aha! so that's it!" reaction, a kind of gut-level "yes." If we must force ourselves to accept an interpretation by an intellectual effort or trick, we can be sure the interpretation has missed the mark. In short, the unconscious, which has produced the dream in the first place, also knows when it has been correctly understood.

There is also the fact that other dreams will comment upon the way interpretations have been given. When dreams are being correctly understood they will tend to change. When the same motif is presented again and again it indicates the message is either being missed, or the individual is not willing to change. It is then as though the unconscious is saying, "You don't get the message so here it is again." Sometimes the dreams are quite explicit about bungled dream interpretations. I recall one woman who thought I was a god and could make no mistakes, but then a dream came in which someone said, "The young doctor is getting the telephone messages wrong." Then I knew I was missing the messages of her dreams.

Sometimes, of course, we simply do not understand the dream. When this happens, it is far better to acknowledge our ignorance than to feel compelled to come up with an interpretation. We can simply say, "Let's just admit we do not understand that dream and hope the unconscious will find another way to phrase the message." It is important that the analyst not feel he or she has to know everything, and that both analyst and client accept the fact that they are often going to be in the dark. It is as though the unconscious appreciates such honesty and then proceeds to find another way to make itself understood.

In order to analyze the dreams of someone else it is crucial that we must have undergone our own analysis. This is not to say that people who have not undergone analysis cannot be helpful to each other, but certainly for the professional who wishes to work with dreams it is essential that he or she have long experience with his or her own dreams. We learn the most about dreams from seeing the meaning and structure of our own; there is no way to get to the meat of the matter without such first hand experience. Also, we are not in a position as therapists to guide someone else through the dark passages of the unconscious if we have not been there ourselves.

Oddly enough, few schools of psychiatry and psychology require personal analysis of those persons who will eventually become therapists. Personal analysis, however, is at the center and heart of the training to become a Jungian analyst. In fact, persons are not even considered for Jungian training until they have had extensive analysis, and personal analysis continues to be at the core of the work of the future analyst throughout his or her training.

If we are able to share our dreams with an experienced and properly trained professional, that is a fine thing, but many times that will not be possible, and then we will have to do what we can on our own. Fortunately there are many helpful ways we can approach our dreams even if we do not have an extensive psychological background or an opportunity to consult with someone else. It is to this that we now turn.

Working With Our Own Dreams

If we are on our own with our dreams the first thing we can do is the same as if we were in analysis: we can write them down. This, as mentioned before, is like entering into a contract with our unconscious, besides having the practical value of fixing our dreams in our memory. To do this we will want to keep a journal in which we can record our dreams, our reflections upon them, and other matters that relate to our psychological and spiritual life. A psychological journal is, in fact, a most helpful and useful tool, the most inexpensive form of psychotherapy of which I know. Into the journal go the dreams, the chance thoughts, the creative ideas, the angry, dark moods and thoughts, the conflicts, the fantasies that cross our screen of consciousness. Keeping a journal tends to strengthen the ego, objectify the unconscious in a helpful way, promote a relationship between the

ego and the unconscious, help us not to become overwhelmed and possessed by unconscious forces, and also
promotes creativity by providing a place where creative
thoughts that otherwise might be lost can, as it were, be
planted so that they may take root in us and grow.

Making a habit of recording our dreams brings about a
subtle but significant change in consciousness, even when
we do not understand them. In her novel *Wuthering Heights*,
Emily Bronte has her heroine, Cathy, say of dreams, "I've
dreamt in my life dreams that have stayed with me ever
after, and changed my ideas; they've gone through and
through me, like wine through water, and altered the colour
of my mind."[26] Dreams do "alter the colour" of our minds. It
is difficult to describe the effect dream recall has upon us
because the complexion of consciousness is changed so
gradually and in such a subtle way, but it is like adding
another dimension to our lives. Sometimes the dreams
themselves reflect this. We may dream of finding new rooms
in our house we did not know were there before, or of moving to a larger, more resplendent house; in this way the
dreams express the change that is taking place in us. Or we
may dream of having a swimming pool in our backyard, for
remembering dreams is like containing a little bit of the
water of the unconscious and having it available for our
renewal. Or perhaps we dream of having an aquarium of
beautiful tropical fish, for remembering dreams is like catch-
ing fish, or containing a bit of the life of the sea of the
unconscious.

Emily Bronte, Stevenson, Abraham Lincoln, Dostoevsky,
and many other creative people remembered their dreams
long before the era of depth psychology. Perhaps it was the
attention they gave their dreams and their inner life that was
at least partly responsible for their great energy and creativity. Remembering dreams is like irrigating a field, watering
a garden, or planting seeds in the ground.

The next step we can take with our dreams after record-

---

[26]Emily Bronte, *Wuthering Heights*, edited by David Daiches, Penguin Books,
Baltimore, Maryland, 1961, p. 120.

ing them is to walk around in them, and, as James Hillman
of Zurich once put it, "make a friend" of them. The dream,
as we saw in the previous section, is like a story, and we can
explore the dream story, ruminate about it, ponder it, and
re-experience it, just as we might savour or reflect upon
experiences in our outer lives. As I indicated in the discussion of dreams in therapy, one role of the analyst is often to
assist the dreamer to walk around in his or her own dream.
If we are on our own, we will have to do this for ourselves.
Asking ourselves questions will help. "How did I feel in the
dream? What was it like when the various dream events
occurred? How did such-and-such a dream figure impress
me? What does this-or-that figure in the dream make me
think of?" And, above all, there is the question, "Why did
this particular dream come to me?" For we must approach the
dream as though it were sent to us by a superior intelligence
for a specific reason or purpose. As we have seen, our dreams
often take up a position that is compensatory to our conscious
life and attitudes. In this way the dream can fulfill or correct
consciousness by adding something to us that was not there
before. If we can find the answer to the question of why this
particular dream came to us, we will have come close to the
point of the dream.

Meditation is another way to work with our dreams;
this takes us a step beyond recording them and mulling
them over in our minds. As with any kind of meditation, we
begin by relaxing our minds and bodies, and freeing ourselves from distractions.[27] We then use a scene, symbol, or
image from a dream as an object of our contemplation.
Meditation upon dreams fixes them more firmly in our
minds, makes them more real to us, and sets in motion a
flow of energy between the conscious mind and the unconscious, with the dream symbols as a bridge.

Meditation upon dreams helps us find more energy for
living because, as we have seen, dreams contain a great deal

---

[27]For a more thorough treatment of meditation than this book allows, see Morton
T. Kelsey's book, *The Other Side of Silence*. The last chapter of my book, *Healing and
Wholeness* also contains a more elaborate description of meditation.

of energy. In such meditations we start the flow going by giving conscious energy or attention to the dreams, then we receive energy back from the life that the dream symbols contain within them. We can think of energy flowing in and out, from the unconscious to consciousness, then back again in a great circle, for energy never stays constant; it is not a static thing, but a flow. The energy we have in consciousness must be used so that new energy may replace it. The unconscious is the great source of our energy. Meditation upon dreams helps us tap into it.

Another method of meditating upon dreams is to paint them. Many dreams invite us to depict them pictorially, and the images of dreams can be pictured in oils, water colors, or whatever other medium seems called for. If we draw, paint, or sculpt our dreams we live with the dream's images, which has the same beneficial effects as I have just described. We also will find that sometimes the painting we have produced reveals details and nuances of meaning that otherwise would have escaped us. Now, with the image of the dream before us in our painting, we can really *see* what that image is. The use of color is often especially beneficial for it brings out the emotional impact and meaning of the dream.

Needless to say, it is not the perfection of the painting that is important, but the process. It does not matter if it is a "good" painting or not, what does matter is that we do it. It is, in fact, often better if we are not a professional artist, for the trained artist will find it exceedingly difficult to get away from the perfectionism of his craft long enough to enter into the spirit of the image he is painting. I once worked with a professional artist who tried painting her dreams but met with failure because her critical, professional side was always there trying to make it into another one of her skilled paintings. I finally suggested that she should paint her dreams with her left hand, for then no one could expect her to produce a painting of artistic merit. This she did not try, but the suggestion did free her to develop two painting styles: a very detailed, perfected style, which she used when painting professionally, and a wild, chaotic style, which she used when just painting for herself. The first paintings were much better technically, but the psychological paintings had more vitality and energy.

A method of working with our dreams that goes a step beyond meditation is active imagination.[28] Active imagination is a technique for relating to the unconscious originally developed by C. G. Jung. It is a powerful and useful tool for working things out with the unconscious on one's own, and is the natural way to go when there is no analyst or spiritual director available, or when a person must go beyond analyzing the contents of the unconscious and work out a relationship to them.

Active imagination takes a manifestation of the unconscious and seeks to enter into a conscious relationship with it. It is *active* because we are entirely awake and active in the process; it is *imagination* because the unconscious is allowed to represent itself to us spontaneously. For simplification, we can talk of the dialogue form and the story form. The dialogue form is the simplest way to begin because much of the time a dialogue is going on in our minds anyway, and we simply begin to write it down and take a more definite role in it. How many times are we dimly aware that something like a running argument is going on in our minds! A "voice," that is, an autonomous train of thought, is speaking with us or bedevilling us within our minds. A very common form of this is the "courtroom scene." Something like a guilt-producing, critical voice is commenting upon us, an Inner Prosecutor, or Great Scorekeeper, who gets on our case and makes us feel inferior or unworthy. This Inner Prosecutor is also a self-appointed Judge. He both accuses us and pronounces judgment upon us. A place to start active imagination would be to write down what this inner Prosecutor is saying to us, then make a definite stand, answering back, and "having it out" with this accusing voice. In this

---

[28]Jung's references to active imagination are scattered throughout his writings. Especially good passages can be found in the *Mysterium Coniunctions*, CW 14, and the *Tavistock Lectures*, CW 18. The indexes of these volumes should be consulted. I have also written a more complete description of this process in the last chapter of my book *Healing and Wholeness*.

way we can begin to come to terms with it. There is also a positive, helpful inner figure, who is experienced by us when we suddenly have a creative, helpful thought. Sometimes, for instance, a thought may spontaneously occur to us that gives us just the right attitude or counsel in a certain situation. A relationship with this positive, helpful, guiding voice can be developed through active imagination, through recording conversations with this inner Shepherd of our souls. In any case, it is best that the active imagination be written down. This gives it substance and reality, and also strengthens our hand in the work, for writing things down is a prerogative of the ego.

In the story form we might begin with a dream that has not reached a satisfactory conclusion, but has ended abruptly. Or, we could take a dream in which we are dissatisfied with our response to what has transpired in the dream. We then complete the dream by imagining what would happen next and selecting our response to what happens. It is like telling ourselves a story. Of course, there will be a voice within us that will say, "This has no meaning, you are only making this up." We must pay no attention to this voice, but continue our work anyway, writing down whatever occurs to us as we continue to develop the dream as a story. The fact is that the unconscious can give us the images we need as we continue the dream in this way through our imagination. But the experience is different from dreaming because now we are fully awake and we can choose the responses we will make in the imaginative action that is unfolding before us.

We can also begin active imagination with a fantasy, that is, with an autonomous, uninvited piece of imagination that keeps intruding into our consciousness. A sexual fantasy might be such a starting place, or the persistent fantasy in which a burglar is breaking into our house. We write down this uninvited fantasy, but this time we consciously participate in what unfolds. The fact that the fantasy comes of its own accord means that it derives energy from the unconscious, and that there is something purposive about it. By interacting more deliberately with this fantasy in active imagination we have an opportunity to have a better relationship with a vital energy of the unconscious that otherwise might simply obsess us.

We can also begin with a mood or an affect. If we find ourselves in a depressed state of mind, or feeling resentful, this darkness or anger can be personified and we can address ourselves to it and see what it has to say.

These are some suggestions of ways to proceed with active imagination. There are no rules. Anything goes and anything may happen. A dialogue, for instance, might want to turn into a story, or the story ending of a dream might wind up as a dialogue with a dream figure. We may wind up as a very central character doing a lot of the talking, or, we may wish to put ourselves into a dream figure, *be* that figure in our imagination, as it were, and see what it has to say. Or we may do both. The important thing is to enter into the process and see what happens.

In the Bible the story of the Temptations in the Wilderness[29] is a good illustration of active imagination. In this story Jesus *talks to* the devil. He takes that tempting inner voice, personifies it and experiences it as the autonomous reality that it is, and in this way "has it out" with him. In Greek literature, we have the story of Proteus in the *Odyssey*. Proteus is the shape-shifting old-man-of-the-sea who will, however, always tell the truth if you seize him and hold him in spite of the diverse shapes he may assume. That is what active imagination is: seizing and holding the elusive contents of the unconscious and, like Jacob with his angel,[30] demanding that they yield a blessing. It is hard work, and for this reason it is difficult to get people to do it because we are naturally lazy about such things, but it also gives a great return on the energy we expend.

I should point out that there is a slight danger in active imagination, which is that we might start a flow of images from the unconscious and not be able to turn it off. This would create anxiety and confusion. In my experience with

[29]Matthew's Gospel, Chapter 4.
[30]Genesis 32:24-30.

myself and others I have never known this to happen, but it is
a possibility, and for this reason people who are not fairly
conversant with their psyche, or who do not have a spiritual
director to whom they can turn, should be cautious about
using this technique.

Next, of course we can try to interpret our dreams for
ourselves. Here we run into the difficulty of understanding
the symbolism of our dreams, and sometimes, to avoid this,
we tend to take them too literally and concretely. One way to
approach our dreams is to concentrate first upon the basic
idea of the dream, putting aside for the moment its symbolism. For instance, a man dreams of carrying a heavy
weight up a steep hill. Although what he is carrying is a
small object, it is incredibly heavy and he can barely inch
his way along. But then, suddenly, he is at the top; like
magic he is suddenly there with his extraordinarily heavy
burden. The basic idea of the dream might be expressed this
way: "An incredibly difficult task that seems to require all
your strength can suddenly become very easy." In expressing the meaning of the dream this way we have not yet
dealt with any of its symbolism, but we have expressed its
underlying theme.[31] Later we can approach the symbolism
of the dream. The incredibly heavy object often symbolizes
the weight of the Self, of wholeness. *That* is the burden we
must carry, an archetypal motif we find in the legend of
Christopher, who carried a child over the river and, as he
did so, felt the weight on his back become greater and
greater so that he was barely able to stumble across to the
other side. Then, placing his burden down, he saw it was
the Christ whom he had carried.

Getting at the basic idea or theme of the dream is often
helpful, for then we can say, "Is this how I feel? Do I feel as
though I am carrying a tremendous weight? Where in my
life am I doing this?" But ultimately to get at the dream more
completely we will have to understand and relate to its symbolism as well, for the dream could have expressed its basic

---

[31]My thanks to Mark Thurston of Virginia Beach for calling my attention to the
importance of themes in dreams.

idea in many ways, but it chose one particular way. To get at the meaning of our dream symbolism we must begin, of course, by associating to the various parts of our dream in the manner already described. What does this or that make me think of? What does such-and-such a person bring to my mind? Often the process of association will bring up the meaning of the dream symbols and the message of the dream will become clear. But sometimes, especially if the symbols are archetypal in nature, we may want help, and people often ask where they can turn.

Unfortunately I do not know of any good dictionary of symbols. The best source for the meaning of symbols is to be found in the writings of C. G. Jung. The volumes of his *Collected Works* are well indexed, and some of them are particularly useful. Let us say that we dream of a snake, or an unidentified flying object. If we are able to locate a passage in Jung's writings in which these symbols are discussed we may find Jung is commenting upon our dream. Of course we should not follow what Jung says slavishly, for what he is saying in this particular passage may not exactly fit our dream, but we can meditate upon what he says, and this is often surprisingly helpful.

Another useful source for such purposes is Jung's *Visions Seminars*.[32] These volumes have a very useful index. To invest in a set of books such as this is expensive, but no more expensive than eating out at a restaurant or taking a weekend vacation. Becoming conscious always has its price, and if we want it badly enough we will pay the price gladly.

Finally, we want to remember that dreams need to be told. It is the most natural thing in the world to awaken in the morning and say to our wife, husband, or parent, "I had the strangest dream last night." If we tell our dream to someone, we relive the dream as we tell it. The process of telling it amplifies and enlarges the dream images, and also engenders insights into the dream that otherwise might not have come to us. It is much like turning on the water in a

---

[32]C. G. Jung, *Visions Seminars*, Spring Publications, Postfach 190, 8024 Zurich, Switzerland.

faucet. As we do this, water that lay in the pipes below comes to the surface. So in telling our dreams all kinds of insights and associations that lay just below the surface of consciousness emerge into the light.

However, if we are going to tell our dreams to someone it must be the right kind of person, and this means someone who respects the things of the soul and will hear our dreams in the correct way. To tell a dream to someone who will disparage or ridicule it, or who will offer blunt, uninformed opinions about its meaning, will only be destructive. "Neither cast ye your pearls before swine," Jesus said,[33] and the reason for this is that swine cannot tell the difference between pearls and ordinary food so they devour everything.

We may, however, find a trusted friend with whom we can share dreams, or sometimes a husband and wife can talk their dreams over together. Generally speaking, when telling dreams to people, it is best to have an understanding that what we need is someone to listen to the dreams and not to interpret them. We want someone to help us hold the dream and look at it, not someone who feels compelled to offer an answer or opinion. If interpretations *are* offered they should be offered tentatively, as mere suggestions, and not imposed upon the other person. This is especially important because the person who is hearing our dreams may have his or her own blind spots that the dream may touch upon. We may then receive, not an informed interpretation of the dream, but a judgmental opinion that emerges from some hidden, touchy area in the person that the dream has happened to hit upon. The trained professional, hopefully, has been through enough analysis so that he is aware of his blind spots and can keep them from intruding into his clients' material, but this may not be the case with persons who have not had the benefit of such training.

It is also possible for a group of people to discuss dreams and related material. This only works when there is a trust relationship among the members of the group. Dreams may give away our secrets, and if another person

---

[33]Matt. 7:6 KJV.

knows our secrets they may be used against us, especially should such a person have an unrecognized power attitude. It is usually best that no one in the group try to interpret another person's dream. Questions can be asked, helpful suggestions or observations made, but no interpretations, for the value of the group is that it provides a medium in which dreams can be shared with like-minded people. When a group of people try to interpret a dream they usually wind up "picking at it," or a secret competition starts among the members of the group to see who is the most skillful at such things and will come up with the cleverest ideas. The result of all this is more apt to be half-baked opinions than helpful interpretations. But if interpretation can be avoided, members of such a group can be quite helpful to each other.

The natural way of working with dreams, then, is to regard them as an ordinary but important part of everyday life, and share them with meaningful persons. An example of the natural way in which people can relate to dreams is given by the anthropologist Kilton Stewart who, in 1935, visited a remote group of Malayan natives, the Senoi Indians. Stewart was greatly impressed by these people because of their democratic way of life, and the fact that they lived without a police force, psychiatric hospitals or the equivalents, or war. The key to their harmonious life, Stewart concluded, lay in the way they dealt with their dreams.

Dream interpretation belonged to everyone in the Senoi community. It is true there were specialists in dreams, the *halaks*, who were certain individuals especially chosen by the spirits for this vocation, but basically dreams were a matter of community life. "Breakfast in the Senoi house," Kilton Stewart wrote, "is like a dream clinic." People listened to and discussed the dreams of children, husbands, wives, and friends. The Senoi believed that hostile images that appeared in dreams had the effect of turning a man against himself and others. In dreams a man had the capacity to see the nature and effect of these hostile figures, and the opportunity therefore to deal with them. Unless the hostile dream figures were related to, the negative dream environment would be reproduced in outer society and life, or a person would become separated from his own Self.

Fortunately, it was always possible for a person to change his dream environment by properly relating to his dream figures. The dream figures represented real spiritual forces that came for a purpose and to which a person could relate. If they were hostile, it was because something in the dreamer created such a state. Everything that came in a dream was believed by the Senoi to have a purpose, and the way the dream figures were acting had its own significance. "Dream characters are bad," Stewart summarizes, "only as long as one is afraid and retreating from them, and will continue to seem bad and fearful as long as one refuses to come to grips with them."

The Senoi believed dreams were the natural way in which their inner spiritual forces contacted them, and that dreams were meant to be recognized, discussed, and understood. Dreams belonged to everyone and were not reserved for the mental specialist to use in treating people who were sick. Rather, dreams were used to keep from getting sick, and were used in ordinary life as a way to maintain psychological and social health.[34]

The dream theory of the Senoi Indians closely resembles many of the ideas of Jungian psychology. The idea, for instance, that a person should make peace with the figures of his dreams and come to terms with them parallels the idea we mentioned before; i.e., that the unconscious turns toward us a reflection of the face we turn toward it. Modern psychology agrees with the Senoi that it is our task, through patience, self-understanding, humility, and a willingness to change, to come to terms with the figures of our dreams, recognize them as parts of ourselves, and seek to establish a relationship with them. Truly we create our own devils through our ignorance, self-rejection, fear, and narrow-mindedness. Like the Senoi, Jung also sees the dream as a guide for the soul and a way to preserve and maintain health, not simply as a treatment for those who are ill.

---

[34]See Kilton Stewart's article, "Dream Theory in Malaya," Chapter 9 in the book, *Altered States of Consciousness*, edited by Charles T. Tart; John Wiley and Sons, 1969.

The Senoi Indians had a "dream culture," dreams were incorporated into the everyday life of the whole people and became part of the social fabric. In this respect, they were like the American Indians who also relied greatly upon their dreams, and believed they were sent by the Great Spirit to guide the soul in this life.

Our present Western civilization is spiritually starved. Our material and technological progress has far outstripped our spiritual progress. If anything, the spiritual condition of Western man is worse than ever, as is evidenced in the widespread wars, crime, and psychological and other illnesses that characterize our times. Jesus declared, when Satan tempted him to use his spiritual powers to turn stone into bread and feed a starving mankind, "Man shall not live by bread alone, but by every word that proceedeth out of the mouth of God."[35] It is simply a fact that man's soul needs daily nourishment, and when it is empty the human condition suffers. Alcohol is no substitute for the living word of God that we all crave, and an empty house is an open invitation for all manner of devils to enter in and possess us. The time has come to reorient ourselves, to look within as well as without, and to accept the reality of the unconscious as a partner in our lives. Then we can incorporate dreams as a way to receive the word of God into our souls; we can be filled with spiritual food. The time has come for nothing less than a radical cultural change, and the kind of spiritual renewal that only a recognition of the unconscious, and the dreams through which it speaks, can provide.

How it might work if we developed such a dream culture in our own country is shown in the next section of this book in which we study the dreams of the young man who was mentioned in the Introduction. As I said there, one interesting thing about this short series of dreams is that this young man was not in any kind of therapy. He made good use of his own dreams by recording them, and reacting to them instinctively. For this reason, in addition to the educational value these dreams have because of their striking content, they show us what it might be like if following our dreams were part of our cultural heritage.

---

[35]Matt. 4:4 KJV.

MARTIN'S DREAMS

Dream 1

I have already pointed out that dreams are tailor-made to the individual, and reflect the psychological and life situation in which the dreamer finds himself. Martin's first dream is a good example of this. Martin is 20 years old at this time. It is early summer and he is between his sophomore and junior years at a large Midwestern university where he has been doing well. He will return to school in late summer, but he has made a decision: he will not return to the usual dormitory facilities of the university, but will live with a group of other students in what is to be an experiment in communal living. After he has reached this decision he has the following dream:

"Early in the morning, with the dawn, I arise. The stillness of the hour is full of anticipation. I am excited. The dawn holds for me the promise of an important day. The early morning hours come, and bring with them purpose and strength. They are also hours of confidence; I am confident. Still no one else in the house has awakened. My father still sleeps, my brothers and sister still sleep.

"I leave the house to be refreshed by the morning air. Outside, I expand into the space about me. The air and I are as one. There is joy.

"The return to the house is necessary. I realize that I must make the return although it will in part be un-

69

pleasant for I foresee what it is that I must do and at first
it will be difficult.

"At the door of the house my father waits, stern
and stiff. He is himself as a door. The house has awakened; all is ready now. I approach. I am silent. Confidence is still with me. A few feet short of the door I stop
and slowly begin to raise my head, which had been
lowered as I approached the door. I meet my father's
eyes. For a second he braces himself. Then, with pain,
he steps aside. His eyes are now those of a weeping
boy. I pass through beside him. I realize that this must
be. I realize that I can do nothing for my father. He must
weep alone. His son could never be capable of drying
his tears.

"Inside the house the children have been waiting.
They were quiet as they saw me pass through the door
beside my father. Now they are waiting on me. They
watch me with expectant eyes.

"I motion. They arise. I smile. They laugh gently,
cautiously. Then, turning, I walk to the door and they
follow.

"As the last of them pass through the threshold it is
as if some evil spell which the house held over the children at last has been broken for at once they come alive
with dance and song and I too am filled with a bound-
less joy. I dance about them all, hugging them and lift-
ing them high above my head. They laugh with glee
and dance and jump and sing some more.

"The sounds of their happiness only increase as I
lead them from the yard to the road and down the road
to the house of the beautiful young lady."

Clearly the dream seems to affirm Martin in his decision. The atmosphere of the dream is light, positive, joyful,
life-giving. The dream seems to say, "In making your own
choice in this matter you have taken a step toward freedom
and independence." If we did not know of the decision that
Martin made just prior to the dream we would be baffled; so
the dream is a good example of the point made earlier, that it

is important to know the circumstances of a person's life if
we are to understand that person's dreams.

Dreams are often important in helping us make decisions. They frequently offer us valuable hints about which
way we should go in life, although they do not write out a
message in bold letters proclaiming what we should do.
Dreams do not make choices for us. Making decisions is part
of the work of the ego, and people who turn the decision-
making process entirely over to the unconscious are usually
disappointed, and, sometimes, make the wrong choices.
There is a tendency in most of us to avoid "biting the bullet," and to shirk the hard choices that must be made in life.
We want God, or dreams, or prayer, or someone else to do
that difficult thing for us. We can expect to find guidance
from our dreams, but at some point we must choose and be
responsible for our choice. Otherwise we would not mature.
However, after a decision has been made a dream will often
comment upon it. In this case, the dream may have given
Martin this affirmation of his decision in order to help him
overcome any lingering doubts, and to strengthen his courage to enter his new life.

But there is much more in the dream than this, of
course. For instance there is the matter of his father. Martin
says of his father that he was an unhappy man who perhaps
still carried an injury from childhood when his own parents
were divorced. Being the father of seven children, he naturally had to work extremely hard; as he disliked his work
this was a great source of pain for him. He often said that he
only worked as a business executive because he had to in
order to support his family, but he really wished to be a
writer or reporter, so it can be said that he lived a kind of
sacrificial life. However, when we sacrifice a part of our
genuine self, no matter how noble the reason, there is always a negative effect, for that life energy in us that is being
denied turns sour and creates a bad atmosphere. So Martin's
father created a bad atmosphere in the household, and his
relationship to Martin and the other children lacked
warmth. Perhaps his unconscious resentment over having
to sacrifice so much of himself interfered with his ability to
relate more closely to his children. At any rate, Martin was

closer to his mother than to his father, and partly because of the tension with his father he wanted to leave home as quickly as he could. Yet at the same time he felt sympathy for his father. Martin disliked his father only because his unhappiness infected the whole family, but he kept a warm place in his heart for him because he seemed to understand the impossible situation in which his father found himself.

The father is in the dream and not the mother (though she appears later) because in making his decision Martin had to go against his father's wishes. His father was very opposed to his son's plan to live in a commune. To him, people who lived in communes were communists, and communists represented everything devilish. We need to remember that all of this took place in the late 1960's, at the height of the Vietnam war, when there was considerable tension between the generations, and the matter of communism was an exceedingly divisive factor between many parents and their children. The father was a determined man so it took a good deal of resoluteness and rebellion on Martin's part to defy him.

So when the dream speaks of Martin's returning to the house, seeing his father waiting stern and stiff, and having to pass by him and bring out the children, even though it leaves his father weeping, we can take this as a comment about what Martin must do in relationship to his father: he must go his own way, get past his father and out into life, and not be swayed by fear of his father, nor by his sympathies for him. Martin is a sensitive young man and it is not easy for him to cause his father pain, but in the dream he does not give in to this, nor does he let feelings of guilt dissuade him from the course he must follow. Martin commented on this dream that his father upheld an American middle-class life style with the help of a "ghetto Catholic mentality." He noted rather sympathetically, "To have your son reject what you think is the best thing which you can give him is no easy thing to handle."*

Earlier we spoke of the archetypes. The separation of a

---

* As noted in the introduction, comments from Martin in quotation marks are taken directly from our correspondence about his dreams.

child from his or her parents is an archetypal situation; that is, a typical and crucial life situation that has been repeated over and over billions of times. It is essential that such a transition take place. If a young man or woman clings too long to father or mother, his or her life does not develop correctly; life is cheated because of the childish attitude that refuses to give up the safety and protection of the parents. Such a young person ultimately pays the price for refusing to grow up and become independent by an early death, a sexual maldevelopment, or some other symptom that indicates there is a profound disturbance in the life energies.

Primitive people marked archetypal times in life with appropriate rituals. For a boy or girl whose time had come to enter into adult life there were the puberty rites. These rites-of-passage helped the young boy or girl to become a man or woman by facilitating the transition from childhood to maturity; they helped sever the psychological umbilical cord that links a child to parents, home, and childhood, and led the young person into adult life.

The form of the puberty rites varied from one group to another, and those for girls differed from those for boys. With girls, for instance, the transition was usually made at the time of the first menstruation, and the rite usually centered around instructions in woman's mysteries and lore. In one tribe, the young girl had to spend many days in seclusion in a dark hut in the forest. She should not see the sun, and the sun's rays should not fall upon her, for this was the hostile masculine power, but the moonlight did her no harm. In the case of boys, the rites involved tests of psychological and physical endurance that inculcated the virtues of masculine ego stability, as well as the revelation to the young man of a secret knowledge known only to the men of the tribe. In some cases, as with the American Plains Indians, there was a quest the young man or woman undertook for a guiding dream or vision that would give a spiritual identity. After the Vision Quest was completed the young person received a new name based upon what had been revealed in the vision; the childhood name was no longer used.

Puberty rites always involved the physical separation of

the child from the parents, especially the mother. The boy was taken away from the parental home to a remote spot, and after the conclusion of the rites was not permitted to live again with his parents. In one Australian tribe the climax of the ritual came when the young man, now fully initiated, returned to the village and his mother asked him for a drink. Instead of giving her a drink, however, he threw the water upon her. The mother then withdrew to her own camp, crying for her son as if he were dead, while the young man went to live with the other men.

This action seems brutal, but its brutality is mitigated by the fact that it was a prescribed ritual, hence an impersonal act that both mother and son understood. It is far less brutal than the way some of our young people have to act today in order to separate themselves from their parents. Driven unconsciously by the same archetypal need that underlies the ancient puberty rites, many a young man or woman today has shed psychological blood in order to separate from the parents.

As a result, parents and children are often left with painful wounds. The parents feel rejected, bitter, and resentful because after their years of sacrifice their child turns on them. The child is also resentful, sensing somehow that the parents have emotional ties that are holding him back. The more unconsciously all of this is played out the more painful are the wounds.

Mythology and religious lore contain many examples of such child-parent separations. In the New Testament we have the story of Jesus who, as a boy of twelve, was taken to the temple. When the time came for his parents, Mary and Joseph, to return home they couldn't find him. They finally discovered him talking with the elders of the temple and, naturally, were angry with him for his seeming callousness toward them. Jesus simply answered, as though surprised at their lack of understanding, "Did you not know that I must be busy with my Father's affairs?"[1] Here we have the denial of the parents, the revelation to the young boy of the higher

---

[1]Luke: 2:49

knowledge of spiritual things, and the substitution of the
relationship with the biological parents for a relationship
with the spiritual parent. The elders act in the role of initiators in the story, the spiritual figures who attend the
young boy or girl in this time of transition, for the biological
parents can never be the spiritual initiators for the son or
daughter. It is also interesting that this is the only story we
have of Jesus' life before he began his ministry as a mature
man. This suggests the importance of this time of transition.

A tale from mythology that parallels Martin's first
dream, with its motif of the father who is left weeping, is
found in the story of Parsifal, the hero of the Legend of the
Holy Grail.[2] Parsifal's father and brothers were killed as
knights, so his mother took him as a small boy to live with
her alone in the forest where he would not have a chance to
enter such a dangerous profession. But one day when Parsifal was a young man he saw five splendid horsemen riding
through the forest in the glorious regalia of knighthood. He
was fascinated, and succeeded in finding out who they
were. As soon as he did so he announced to his mother his
determination to become a knight himself. Nothing his
mother could say dissuaded him, and Parsifal left to seek his
fortune at King Arthur's court, while his mother wept alone.
He never saw her again, for not long after this she died.

The separation of the child from the parent can be one
of life's cruel moments, but this pain is nothing like the pain
that will occur if the separation is not successfully accomplished, for then, as we mentioned, the purposes of life are
thwarted and the price to be paid for this is high. But if the
separation can be accomplished, and parents and children
alike see its necessity, an entirely new relationship can be
established. Many a parent has found that the child who had
seemingly become an enemy during adolescence has become a good friend once maturity has been reached.

All of this is the archetypal background to the dream.
The dream refers to the actual relationship of Martin to his

---

[2]Cf. the interesting discussion of the legend in *HE!*, by Robert Johnson, the
Religious Publishing Company, King of Prussia, Pa., 1974.

personal father on the one hand, but, on the other hand, it refers to the archetypal event, the separation from his parents, taking place within Martin. In this way a dream weaves inner and outer, personal and archetypal, into a single pattern.

We also notice in the dream how active the dreamer is; in fact, he is the crucial figure and occupies the center of the stage. Thus the dream focuses upon the importance of the ego in this particular psychological situation, for without the crucial decision that Martin made, the happy events of the dream could not have transpired.

No doubt it is because of the positive attitude that Martin adopted toward his life that the dream begins with the proclamation of a new day. "Early in the morning, with the dawn, I arise," is the opening line of the dream. Thus a new birth of the young man's life is symbolized, for the dawn symbolizes new life, while the emerging sun that the dawn brings hints at the emergence of the Self that can carry him successfully through life.

All of this exemplifies the "as if" language of dreams. The dream says, "It is *as if* a new day now dawns in this person's life." In this way dreams are like Jesus' parables, for Jesus also spoke an "as if" language. In Matthew's Gospel he begins many of his parables with the words, "The kingdom of heaven is like . . . " which is a way of saying, it is *as if* the kingdom of heaven were a pearl of great price, or a man who discovered a treasure hidden in a field, or a woman who puts the yeast in the bread. Many dreams that otherwise might baffle us will yield their meaning if we keep their symbolic "as if" quality clearly in mind.

The dream shows that Martin is ready to venture out in this brand new day, but first he has to return to the house for the necessary task of freeing the children. Martin tells us that at first these children were his siblings, but later in the dream they were an unknown group of young boys and girls. So the dream makes a contrast between the stern, stiff father, and the young, free children. Martin did not actually take his siblings with him when he went to the University, nor involve any unknown children in his venture, so the children in the dream must symbolize elements of Martin himself. He frees something in himself that is young, growing, and full of potential, from the domination of an inner stern father.

But it is not just the personal father from whom the children must be freed, but also the father as senex. The *senex* and *puer* are two archetypal patterns of masculine development. *Puer* means boy; we usually speak of the "puer aeternus," the eternal boy or youth, such as Peter Pan. *Senex* means "old man"; it is the same word from which we derive our word "senile." The puer is the archetype of eternal youth, and the senex represents the archetype of the old man. As men develop they tend to gravitate more toward one pole or the other; that is, to be shaped more by the puer spirit or by the senex spirit. The puer tends to remain young, changing, and sometimes creative. But he has negative qualities too: the puer tends to refuse maturity, responsibility, commitment, and hard work, especially if it involves drudgery. The puer is close to the feminine in himself; in fact, men who are puer aeterni have a special kind of mother complex. They are often charming, interesting, creative spirits, but it all comes to nothing unless they learn to mature and work. In contrast the senex is strong where the puer is weak. A man moulded by the senex assumes responsibility, works hard, and accepts commitments, but if a man is too shaped by the senex he too develops negative qualities. He then becomes rigid, narrow, inflexible, humorless, and unrelated to the feminine side of life. It is almost superfluous to point out that puer and senex dislike each other intensely.

We call the puer and senex archetypes because they exist in every man and tend to shape the way he develops. Too close an identity with either archetype has its undesirable results. No one wants a man who will not grow up, nor does anyone want a man who loses his heart and youthful spirit. The proper course of development is for a man to steer his way between these opposites, taking the best values of each. If a man tends to the puer side he needs to learn to work, for this is the antidote for every puer. If he veers toward the senex side he needs to learn to play, for this is his antidote.

Martin has lived in the stern but cheerless atmosphere of the senex. Apparently his father was such a man. He lived by work, commitment, and duty, but lost touch with the other side of life.* Martin has to free himself from the domination of this spirit, and succeeds in doing so in the dream. By leading out the children he frees the puer energies in him, which the dream represents as a very positive event. As we shall see later, however, Martin goes too far in the direction of the puer and a corresponding psychological compensation has to be made.

The dream has an interesting ending, for we are told that as Martin and the children go happily out of the house they go "down the road to the house of the beautiful young lady." In myths and fairy tales the prize that the young hero wins for his heroic action is often represented as a beautiful maiden. In this "beautiful young lady" we can recognize the *anima*; that is, the soul figure of a man that we have already briefly mentioned.

No man is entirely masculine; in the unconscious there is a feminine component to his personality that is, naturally enough, personified in his dreams as a woman. Jung gave the name "anima" to this personification of a man's feminine qualities, and felt that she acted as his soul because if he was able to relate to her she introduced him to his unconscious personality and guided him through those psychological changes he must undergo in order to become whole. A young man who has not freed himself from his childishness has a mother or witch figure for an anima image. However, a young man who has exercised the necessary courage to get out into life wins the prize of the anima as a beautiful feminine being. The appearance of the beautiful young lady in Martin's dream emphasizes the creative nature of his psychological development at this point and bodes well for his future.

---

* However, Martin makes the interesting comment that his father also had much of the natural puer in him, but suppressed this tendency. This may be why in the dream Martin leaves him as a "weeping boy."

However, the path of psychological development is never a smooth one and, as we shall soon see, Martin had to experience some dark and chastening times if the promise of this dream was to be realized. Dreams often represent promises or possibilities instead of actualities; that is, some dreams seem to say, "This is the way it is now with you." Other dreams say, "This is the way things can be with you now if you go the proper way in life." Only the context of the dream can tell us which way a dream is to be taken. In this dream there is a matter-of-fact quality: this is what has now been accomplished. But the end of the dream suggests a possibility: "You are moving toward the house of your soul," it says, "but you are not yet there."

It is important to keep this in mind when we look at our dreams. They do not represent fixed and fatalistic events, for always there is the element of choice. The effect of a "bad" dream can be averted by the correct change in conscious attitude, and the hopefulness of a "good" dream can be lost if we do not persevere in the correct direction. This element of choice extends to even the dream experience itself. Martin himself noted, "Within the dream series I was always quite aware of the freedom to decide or not decide in a given situation. It was for me one of the most mysterious aspects of the dreams since I thought that within dreams one was more often than not compelled to follow a certain course of action. A kind of force that was completely undeniable was absent in the dream."

Dream 2

The second dream in our series came in August. By now Martin had left home and had been living in the commune. He notes that at the time this dream came he was becoming disillusioned with the communal experiment; it seemed that he was the only one who cared whether the dishes were washed and the bathroom was clean. The dream was as follows:

"I am alone in the desert. It is midday and the sun high overhead shines on the distant mountains and the cactus about me. The intense light of the sun fills the mountains and the cactus with an uncanny beauty. I could lose myself in contemplating them.

"Suddenly, before me, close to me, between myself and the mountains which only a second ago I was looking at, stands an old Indian chief. He looks towards the sun and his face shines as the sun. The lines on his face tell of hard years and deep wisdom gained through them.

"Just as suddenly, I realize that he is listening; that I am not alone with him in the desert. There is with us a Spirit to Whom the Indian is listening. I do not know how to listen as this old Indian does. I know only that there are three beings present and that the ground is sacred.

"The old Indian does not speak. I dare not question."

This dream is an experience in itself, an example of what Robert Louis Stevenson meant when he said that a man who counted his dreams among his memories was richer than a man who remembered only the events of his outer life. This dream made a deep impression on Martin. He recalled feeling awed and grateful, privileged to have been with the Indian Chief on his sacred ground.

The beauty of the dream emphasizes its importance. Often the unconscious produces beautiful dreams in an effort to attract the attention of the dreamer's consciousness. Just as flowers produce beautiful blossoms in order to attract the insects that spread the flower's seeds to distant places, so dreams sometimes assume a beautiful form in order to attract our attention.

Merely having beautiful dreams, however, is not enough, and beautiful dreams in themselves do not mean that a person is necessarily spiritually or psychologically developed. What matters is what we do with our dreams and our lives. I recall a man who had intensely beautiful and meaningful dreams; however, he was a great parasite, a disagreeable man who nursed a series of imaginary illnesses so he would not have to get a job and work. He did nothing with his beautiful dreams and ignored the unconscious no matter how desperately it tried to get his attention.

So Martin's dream is not simply beautiful, it is beautiful for a purpose. The dreamer needs to notice this wise, old Indian of the dream because this wisdom is what he needs. We have already noted that many dreams are compensatory. We get at the meaning of such dreams by asking ourselves, "Why does such a dream come to me at this time?" In this case, is there something Martin lacks that the dream tries to bring to him?

Because of the deeply spiritual and religious nature of the dream it is a fair guess to assume these qualities are what Martin lacks at this time. The dream can be taken as a compensation for the spiritual emptiness of the commune of which Martin has become a part. He relates that the atmosphere there was heavy and intellectual, and that he himself was living very much up in his head. We have already seen that there was a lamentable lack of concern for ordinary cleanliness and order in the house. In deciding to join the commune, Martin had made a positive step in freeing himself from his father and becoming his own man. But this does not mean that the commune in which he now lives, and his own psychological state, are desirable places to remain. So the dream seeks to correct a lack of spiritual depth in Martin and his life by producing a dream of remarkable religious quality.

Nevertheless, there is more than "mere compensation" to the dream. The dream could not have come if there was not in Martin a potentiality for a deep spiritual development. If spiritual development is what is currently lacking, it is also what is possible.

The most striking element in the dream is the figure of the wise, old Indian. Martin had had very little to do with Indians or Indian lore at the time of the dream. He knew no more about them than any young man might have picked up from grade school studies of Indian life, and from cowboy and Indian movies. Nor had Martin ever been to the type of arid, desert country in which the dream is set. Clearly the Indian is a figure of great wisdom and depth, but not a figure born out of Martin's personal life experience.

There is, in fact, nothing in the dream from Martin's personal world. There is no mention of his car, friends, the university, books or anything that belongs to his everyday life. When this occurs in a dream it is an indication that the dream is from the collective unconscious; that is, it contains archetypal symbols and images that come from the deep layers of the unconscious and not from the dreamer's personal life.

The old Indian is the chief feature of the dream. He can be understood as a particular manifestation of the archetype of the Wise Old Man. Life has its own stored up wisdom. Like the human body, the human psyche has existed for millions of years, and embodies a life wisdom that far transcends the meagre wisdom any one individual can acquire through his conscious efforts. This timeless wisdom of the psyche is often personified as the Wise Old Man and is an archetypal symbol.

But why did the dream select the figure of an American Indian to personify this wisdom? C. G. Jung, who treated many Americans as well as Europeans in his long practice of psychotherapy, observed that the American psyche was different from that of the European. White Americans, he felt, had a European conscious structure, with black mannerisms, and with a touch of an Indian soul. The black qualities of white Americans, Jung felt, came from their long association with black people; the two races had affected each other psychologically, each altering the other. (An example is American folk and popular music). But neither the black man nor the white man is the original inhabitant of America. The soil in America is red, the spirit of the land is Indian. Jung felt that this Indian soul quality was now in the American psyche at a very deep level. "The American," he once said, "on account of the fact that he lives on virgin soil, has the Red Indian in him. The Red man, even if he has never seen one . . . (has) got into the American and you will realize that he belongs to a partly coloured nation."[3]

Chief Seattle hinted at this in a famous speech that he made upon signing the final treaty with the white man in which he declared, "When the last Red Man shall have perished, and the memory of my tribe shall have become a myth among the white man, these shores will swarm with the invisible dead of my tribe, and when your childrens' children think themselves alone in the field, the store, the shop, or in the silence of the pathless woods, they will not be alone. . . . At night when the streets of your cities and villages are silent and you think them deserted, they will throng with the returning hosts that once filled them and still love this beautiful land. The White Man will never be alone."[4]

Perhaps it is this level of the psyche from which the dream has emerged, and Martin is thus confronted by an image drawn from the soil of the land. The Indian lived very closely to nature. Chief Joseph of the Nez Perce Indians once remarked that the Indian liked the land the way the Great Spirit had made it; he did not want to change the land the way the white man did. It may be that what Martin needed at this time was a closeness to the land, to nature, and to the natural spirit that the life, lore, and spirit of the Red Man embodies. This certainly would be a fitting compensation for the "headiness" with which Martin is now identified.

The sun is another important symbol of the dream. The dream begins with Martin alone on the desert, and the sun high overhead, shining on the distant mountains and the cactus roundabout with its intense light. The sun often appears in religious lore as a symbol for God, Christ is often represented as the rising sun, and the Aztecs, as we have already seen, regarded the sun as identical with Huitzilopochtli, the god on whom all human welfare depended. Among the American Indians the sun was the representation par excellence of the Great Spirit, and an object of

[3]C. G. Jung, CW Vol. 18, *The Symbolic Life*, "The Travisock Lectures," p. 47.
[4]*Touch the Earth*, compiled by T. C. McLuhan, Promontory Press, New York, p. 30.

prayer and contemplation. The sun is also a particular symbol for the archetype of masculine consciousness, just as the moon symbolizes feminine consciousness. It is as though the Yang power, or masculine consciousness, sees everything in the startlingly clear light of the sun, and the Yin power, or feminine consciousness, sees things in the shimmering light of the moonlight which, as it were, fuses things together, even as the sunlight differentiates things. The sun seems to be a particularly important symbol for Martin at this time, for the first dream began with the image of the dawn arising, which clearly speaks of the rising sun. If Martin's dreams emphasize the importance of the sun it must be because Martin at this time needs this archetype of masculine consciousness and wholeness.

The face of the old Indian shines as the sun. This reflects the numinosity of the experience the old Indian is having. To contact the archetypes of the collective unconscious, and the spiritual world they show forth, is to be in touch with a great numinosum. We will recall from the Bible that when Moses descended from Mt. Sinai after having his conversation with God, his face also shone, so much so that when he returned to the people they were afraid to come near him because the skin of his face shone so intensely.[5] The Gospels also say of Jesus that on the Mount of Transfiguration "the fashion of his countenance was altered, and his raiment was white and glistering."[6] The similarities between the Biblical descriptions of religious experience, and the symbolism of this dream, occur because they have a common archetypal basis.

Martin is fascinated by the figure of the wise, old Indian and greatly drawn to him. He is deeply impressed with the wisdom that the old Indian embodies, and stands in relationship to him as a pupil to his master. The old Indian thus functions in relationship to Martin as an initiator and spiritual guide. In the previous dream we learned of the separation of Martin from his personal father, now we learn of the

---

[5]Exodus 34:29.
[6]Luke 9:29 KJV.

presence within Martin of a spiritual father. This fulfils the archetypal need of a young man for a spiritual guide other than the biological father to assist him in the rite of passage from boyhood to manhood. In this way the dream compensates Martin's outer life situation, and helps put him in touch with what he lacks.

The old Indian is listening to something. We only know that this "something" is a Spirit. The Indian seems in contact with this Spirit, but the dreamer is not. The dreamer can only infer that a Spirit is present, that they are not alone. The fact that the dreamer is not in contact with this Spirit himself suggests that it is something the dreamer is not yet capable of making conscious. An Indian would no doubt have said that the wise, old Indian is listening to "Wakan Tanka," the Great Spirit or Great Mystery, the universal ground of being and source of all life. The Westerner would call this "God." Whatever it is called, it is clear that this Spirit is the source of the old Indian's knowledge, power, and wisdom, and that it is the presence of this Spirit that makes the ground sacred.

To say that something is sacred means that it is numinous. If something is numinous it must be respected, and treated in a special way. So when God spoke to Moses through the burning bush He told him he was standing on holy ground and must remove his shoes. Our present culture has all but lost its sense of the sacred. Everything today is profane, and what might be sacred and holy is dragged down to the level of the banal and ordinary.

The rituals of the church are a good example. In the beginning the Eucharist was a sacred, numinous ceremony; hence if was open only to the initiated. Those not yet initiated into the mysteries of the faith could not witness, much less take part, in a celebration of the Eucharist. Now the Eucharist is increasingly secularized, and to replace the vacuum left by its lost numinosity there are attempts to make it a service of sociability, neighborliness, and conviviality.

Fortunately, Martin is deeply impressed by the sacred quality of this dream, which shows that he has within him the capacity for a religious development and enlarged conscious understanding of the meaning of his life. If in the dream he had ignored the startling events taking place, or had been unaffected by them, it might have been a sign that he lacked the attitude that would be required of him if he was to bring his inner life to fulfilment. The dream illustrates the point that our reactions in our dreams are highly significant. If a fortunate, blessed event takes place in a dream it is important that we have the appropriate reaction; if there is a catastrophe or ominous event, it is also important that we react accordingly. In either case, if we are not affected by the dream event, this probably suggests either a profound unconsciousness, or a pathological lack of conscience and sensitivity. So Martin's humble, interested reaction to the events of his dream is important.

At the very end of the dream it is said, "The old Indian does not speak. I dare not question." It is always important in dreams, as we have seen, to evaluate the dreamer's actions and responses in the dream. So we have the task of evaluating the dreamer's reluctance to ask any questions of the wise, old Indian. When I first looked at this dream I was tempted to argue that Martin should have asked questions of the wise, old Indian and that something was lost when he did not. I was reminded of the Legend of the Holy Grail, in which Parsifal stumbles into the Grail Castle by accident but loses the whole experience because he fails to ask the vital question, "To whom does the Grail belong?" It seemed to me at first that asking questions might have made the whole experience more conscious to Martin, and might have represented the establishment of a conscious relationship between ego and Self.

There was, however, also a doubt, for perhaps the asking of questions at that point might have been impertinent, and so it seemed to Martin himself who wrote, "I was not ready to become conscious of what these things meant. I instinctively knew that to ask a question would not only have been out of place, but wrong. The Indian communicated this through his silence. I was not to violate the sacred silence and the presence of the Spirit with a student's questioning." He went on to note that questions would have tended to reduce the whole experience to an intellectual level, and, as we shall see, there is already the danger in him of a too intellectual approach to the mysteries of life. So I think we can conclude that for Martin, at this time, it was proper that he listen and observe in silence and not intrude upon the sacredness of what he was witnessing with inappropriate questions. As he pointed out, if the old Indian had wished to say something to him he would have spoken.

The doubt over whether or not Martin should have questioned the Indian shows how a dream interpretation can be argued first one way and then another. Convincing arguments can be made on both sides in this case. This shows that there is no fixed method of arriving at dream interpretations, and the final court of appeal is always the dreamer himself and his intuitive, deep-down feeling response. To Martin, it *felt* as though questions would have been wrong, and that is the final court of appeal.

Where there is such a doubt, however, it is always possible to use the technique of active imagination, which we described earlier. In this case, the procedure would be to recall the image of the wise, old Indian, concentrate upon it, and address oneself to the Indian hoping for a reply. Martin relates that he did this, somewhat at my urging, and asked the Indian what his silence meant, and how he, Martin, could have a similar experience. He relates that the Indian's response came quickly: "There was no answer, he simply bowed his head and walked away disappointedly."

An interesting feature of this dream is that Martin will eventually travel to exactly the kind of country this dream describes, and here he will have his crucial experiences. At the time of the dream nothing could have been farther from his consciousness. The dream anticipates something that is still in the future, an example of the kind of "absolute knowledge" that the unconscious sometimes displays. The dream is thus an indication that the unconscious intends something for Martin and wants to prepare him for it. The unconscious does not merely react to consciousness, it also contains a plan for the development of our lives and personalities, and seeks to make this plan a reality.

The dream also shows the religious qualities of the unconscious. To say the unconscious is religious means that it contains those numinous symbols that require our careful attention, that bind or link us to a transcendent goal, and orient us in life. Clearly this dream is very numinous, which, as Jung once said, means it has emotional value.[7] In the presence of such numinosity we experience our creatureliness, humanness, and incompleteness, which, as Professor Rudolph Otto has shown,[8] are the hallmarks of the religious attitude. The religious man takes into careful consideration these numinous symbols and events, feels linked or bound to them, and from them gets a sense of direction in his life.

The derivation of the word "religion" is helpful here. According to the Fathers of the Church, the word derives from the Latin "religare," which means to reconnect, or link back. We could say, then, that the religious person is one who is connected or bound to the process of individuation. Here Christ on the Cross is a prototype. Christ nailed to the Cross, unable to descend from that wooden cross to which he is inexorably fastened, is symbolic of the human ego which, through individuation, is also inexorably bound to the Self and the process of becoming whole, a process from which we cannot escape except at our great peril.

However, Jung says that the word derives from the Latin "religere," which means to go through again, recollect, or think over.[9] But the implication is much the same, for this suggests that the religious person is one who takes into careful consideration all those numinous events, inner and outer, that cross his path, seeking to find their meaning and extract a whole pattern from them.

After this numinous and powerful dream we might expect the next dream to be equally impressive. Instead the next dream is on a much more ordinary level. Life does not stay on its peaks, and after an ascent up a mountain a descent into the valley is inevitable. One can seldom get to the

---

[7]See C. G. Jung, *Letters Vol. II*, p. 371; Princeton University Press.
[8]Rudolph Otto, *The Idea of the Holy*, Oxford University Press, 1950.
[9]Op. cit. p. 272.

top of the ladder by leaping over the rungs that lead upward from below. For most of us the ascent is slow, and we must step on each rung on the way.

Dream 3

Shortly after the opening of the fall semester of the University, Martin dreamed as follows:

"The first semester of the school year is a week old. Already I have lost interest in my courses. I want to travel; to hitchhike away, if only for a weekend.

"Giving way to the wanderlust that is in me I pack my bag with cheese and bread, fasten tight my sleeping bag and head for the toll road entrance.

"It's Friday morning.

"The first car by stops for me. I run up to it and see, when close, that two friends from school are in the car. We exchange greetings. They ask me where I am going and I tell them that I am heading for New Mexico. Chicago is where they are going and they tell me that I'd be welcome to ride that far with them. I decline the offer since it would take me too far out of my way, saying that it should be easy for me to catch another ride. Then the driver, as if he had just heard me telling him that I was heading for New Mexico, asks surprisingly how do I expect to make it there and back for classes on Monday morning. I am a bit confused, for it had not occurred to me that one weekend would not be enough time to hitchhike to New Mexico and back. I shrug my shoulders as if to answer, "Who knows?" They laugh and drive on. Then my attitude changes. "So what!" I say to myself, "I won't mind in the least if I do not make it back in time for classes on Monday morning. And I continue to hitchhike."

We noted in the dream of the wise, old Indian that the setting of the dream was unfamiliar to Martin; it contained nothing from his everyday life. That is not the case with this dream. Here we have references to the University, to toll roads, to his sleeping bag, to bread and cheese, etc. This indicates that this dream is from a different level—closer to the ego and its everyday world—and so we will not find the depth of archetypal symbolism that we found in the preceding dream.

The dream unfolds like a story, showing Martin about to go on a lark, a carefree hitchhiking trip to New Mexico. He has a certain kind of energy in this dream, and it is not hard to recognize this as the energy of the puer. It was this puer energy that was released from the domination of the senex father at the time of the first dream. Now it is in full swing and is leading the young dreamer into a youthful adventure. However, such a trip would create a conflict. How could Martin complete this hitchhiking trip and still get back in time for classes the following Monday morning? The dream represents him as unaware of this conflict until the two friends from school laughingly point it out to him. So the dream has the function of bringing a conflict up into consciousness where the ego must face it and resolve it one way or the other. The two friends play a helpful role in raising this conflict into consciousness. The fact that they laugh as they drive away, leaving Martin with his conflict of conscience, suggests that they personify his shadow, for the shadow personality is free of the usual bounds of conscience that afflict our conscious ego personality. Wherever there is humor the shadow is involved. Indeed it is the shadow in us who laughs, as Harvey Mindess has shown in his fine little book *Laughter and Liberation*.[10]

The focus of the dream, however, is not on the two friends, but on the dreamer, and the choice he must make between his carefree Peter Pan-like adventure on the one hand, and his commitment to the responsibility of school on the other. The dreamer does not experience much difficulty in making his decision. With a shrug of his shoulders he says, "So what! I won't mind in the least if I do not make it

---

[10]Harvey Mindess, *Laughter and Liberation*, Nash Publishing Co., Los Angeles, 1971.

back in time for classes on Monday morning." So much for the demands of the senex side of life! Martin has thrown in his lot with the puer.

At the time of this dream, Martin had no conscious intention of dropping out of school. Two weeks later, however, he did; the dream anticipated a line of development at work in him that led to this action. However, he did not leave at once on a hitchhiking trip, but remained in the same town living in the commune. A trip to New Mexico was far from his mind at the time, although, as mentioned before, he does within a few months undertake exactly such a journey. So the dream anticipates a plan of action of which Martin is totally unaware. The unconscious has its own plans, and, even though he does not know it, Martin is being guided by his dreams. Slowly but surely he is led to fulfil an inner plan of which he only gradually and imperfectly becomes conscious.

The conflict between the freedom of movement a hitch hiking trip represents for a young man, and the responsibility of school, is a genuine one. There are values on both sides. The importance of education for a bright young man such as Martin is obvious; without it he cannot hope to find his proper place in our society. On the other hand, young people need experiences, and school is more like an exercise in life than life itself. Many young people today suffer psychological deprivation because it is hard for them to find experiences of real life. Alexander the Great ruled the civilized Western world at the age of 20, but in our culture 20 year olds are regarded as still wet behind the ears. Looked at in this way, Martin's instinct in the dream to seek experiences on the open road has something healthy in it.

As mentioned before, Martin did not take his dreams to a counselor, nor was he in any kind of therapy. What would have happened if he *had* been in counseling and had shown this dream to a therapist? A competent therapist would have seen that the dream was exposing a conflict that was just below the threshold of consciousness and would have brought this conflict out into the open. In doing this the therapist might have weighted the scale in favor of staying in school, particularly if he had been a counselor in the service of the University. For while therapists are usually trained to be objective, and not to impose their ideas or convictions on their clients, it remains a fact that they do have their own value systems, and are subject to certain external pressures as well. Thus a counselor who works for the church may feel a certain pressure to return people to the faith, whether that is indicated for them from within or not, and a counselor in the service of a school may feel a pressure to encourage students to remain in the school. It takes a good deal of consciousness and fortitude on the part of therapists to avoid exerting an open or subtle pressure on their clients to adopt certain courses of action which make them look good, or avoid distressing conflicts with external or internal authorities.

It is conceivable that under such an influence Martin might have remained in the University; then he would not have had the adventures that led him in a few months to a transforming experience, and that would have been a great loss. Perhaps it was a good instinct that led him at this time not to seek counseling, but to experience life on his own. There are times to analyze life, and times to live life, and times to live life and analyze it at the same time. At this time Martin was to live his life. Yet he *did* have a counselor, the inner guidance of his dreams, which, even though not understood psychologically, nevertheless influenced him because he took the trouble to record them, and allowed himself to be influenced by them instinctively.

It is good Martin had his dreams, for leaving the University, with no other plan for his life, could have had unfortunate consequences. Not every school dropout succeeds, as Martin did, in finding his way; many have become casualties. This is certainly the fear Martin's parents must have had when they learned their son had left school. His father especially must have been both angry and anxious, full of thoughts such as, "I told you so, I knew that when he joined those communists he would go down the drain." They had no way of knowing, of course, that everything that was happening to him was part of a meaningful plan or purpose.

Like most parents they could only anguish at the seeming confusion, futility and danger, into which their son was evidently moving. Perhaps they were filled not only with despair for him, but also flagellating themselves with guilt. "What kind of parents can we be?" they might have asked themselves when their son seemed to be turning out so "badly." They did not need to feel guilty. There are secret purposes at work in the children that have nothing to do with the parents, but are part of the young person's own underlying life meaning.

I pointed out the obvious when I drew attention to the lack of deep archetypal symbolism in this dream, especially when compared to the previous one. Nevertheless, it is not without its own archetypal quality. For instance, in the dream Martin is reminiscent of a certain type of fairy tale hero. In many fairy tales the hero appears as a guileless, naive fellow who casts commitments aside, and sallies forth into the world with no particular destination, but just for the hell of it to see what will happen. Rather than remaining securely at home, such a hero ventures into the world with a naive curiosity that is exactly the kind of attitude that leaves him open to creative experiences from within and without. This sort of hero is refreshingly free of exploitive ego motives. He is not trying to "find God," or reach any sublime spiritual height, or arrive at any particular goal, but is simply open to life. As Marie-Louise von Franz points out in her analysis of this kind of hero, "This is a good precondition for the heroic action"[11] In the dream, Martin is exactly this kind of fairy tale hero, which means that he is following a creative archetype within himself, fulfilling the pattern most likely to lead him to a larger life experience. Yet it all could have turned out badly, for there is a narrow line between the guileless hero who discovers life, and the nihilistic and frivolous youth who, having cast aside tradition and security, is destroyed by evil because he does not have inner protection and guidance. Of course there would be no such heroes at all if there were not the dangers.

---

[11]My thanks to Gilda Frantz of Los Angeles for pointing this out to me.

In spite of its seemingly superficial quality, therefore, the dream has deep roots. Martin was led, as I mentioned, to leave the University two weeks after this dream, so the first part of the dream was fulfilled, but he did not yet undertake a journey. Instead of hitchhiking to New Mexico he remained where he was, living in the commune, and here he stayed even as Christmas drew near. Then he had his fourth dream.

Dream 4

The fourth dream:

"I had worked long and hard on building my room in the basement of the house. For three weeks I had worked on it, sweeping, washing, and painting the floors and walls, building a desk, table, chair, bed and doorway, putting in a window, and laying a carpet. I liked the room hidden there in what had been a dusty, dirty room full of all kinds of junk in the basement. My work had caused a real transformation. When I started, no one else in the house thought it possible to make the room livable. I surprised them; I amazed them. For three weeks, every day, all day, I worked with my hands on the room and it was all my own doing. I did like the room very much, and now all of these people whom I did not know were screaming at me, commanding me to give my room up.

"I could not understand why. There did not seem to be any reason why I should be made to give up my room. But there they were, all of these people screaming at me to give it up. All of them were screaming at me from above as I stood bowed, dejected in the middle of my room. I tried to reason with them. I pleaded with them that I had transformed wasted space into a livable room. If anything, I said, they should be grateful to me for doing this.

"They were not moved by my pleas. They screamed the louder, and finally, broken under the great force of their relentless opposition, I fell to the floor and gave up my room."

In fact, Martin's room in the commune was in the basement and he had transformed it into a livable place. The image the dream gives of his working on his room is factual. But now in the dream he is being made to give it up, and he cannot understand why.

We have already noted that it is important to notice the way the dream ego responds to the dream situation. In this case, this response is the focus of the dream. Shall the dreamer give up his room or not? Inexorably, the dream forces the dreamer to make a choice; all the forces of the dream converge on the importance of this single decision. We are left with the question, "Did the dreamer make the correct choice?" Was his decision to give up his room a good one, or did it represent a regression?

Our first sympathies are with the dreamer's anguish. Why should he have to give up this room that he toiled so hard to bring to this livable state? The relentless voices pressing upon him to give up his room seem cruel and arbitrary. We are inclined to groan with dismay when we learn that he finally surrendered to these demanding voices, seemingly crushed by them.

The beautiful and well furbished room suggests that the dreamer had reached a certain positive psychological state. A room or house often symbolizes the psychological framework out of which we are living; it is our psychic house in which we dwell. This is clear in Jesus' parable of the two houses, one founded upon rock and one upon sand: "Therefore, everyone who listens to these words of mine and acts on them will be like a sensible man who built his house on rock. Rain came down, floods rose, gales blew and hurled themselves against that house, and it did not fall: it was founded on rock. But everyone who listens to these words of mine and does not act on them will be like a stupid man who built his house on sand. Rain came down, floods rose, gales blew and struck that house, and it fell; and what a fall it had!"[12] Jesus is using a house in this parable as a

---

[12]Matthew 7:24-27.

psychological symbol and our dreams often use dwelling places in much the same way.

If, then, Martin's fine room represents a positive psychological framework he has succeeded in constructing for himself, we must look suspiciously at the voices commanding him to give this up. Perhaps they are collective voices; that is, representations of collective opinion, which are trying to defeat his efforts to improve himself and his place in life, and to which he finally succumbs. There certainly is such a thing as the voice of collective opinion; it does influence us, and is often represented in our dreams. What others think, the general opinions around us, have a way of getting into us and carrying on an autonomous life of their own greatly influencing us from within. We are social beings and the opinions and expectations of our fellows have a powerful effect upon us. Many of us have denied our better side in order to go along with collective attitudes and be one of the group, often without even knowing it.

If the dream had said that the voices that wanted him to give up his room were the voices of Tom, Dick, and Harry, friends in the commune perhaps, we might have viewed them as personifications of the collective attitudes at work in him. In that case we might have seen the dream as representing the way Martin was giving up something of his own because he could not withstand the collective pressure. But the dream says quite specifically that the voices were from "all of these people whom I did not know." Unknown people in our dreams represent what is unknown in us, that is, the voices of the unconscious or the Self. If this is the case, these voices represent an *inner* demand that Martin give up what he has now and move on. They personify a relentless "call" from within, a summons from a Will greater than that of his ego that must be obeyed, even as Moses *had* to obey the Voice that spoke to him through the burning bush, and Jonah was relentlessly pursued by God until he went to Nineveh.

It proves impossible to reason or plead with these voices. In vain Martin argues that he has transformed wasted space into a livable room; in vain he pleads that he has this good place to live and does not want to move. He cannot even cajole them into agreeing that they should be grateful to him for his hard work. Nothing will satisfy these voices except that he give up his room and move on.

So Martin does give up his room. In the light of the dreams that follow it will be clear that this was the correct choice. The good room described by the dream does represent something of positive psychological value. But it is not the best. Jung once wrote, "For the unconscious always tries to produce an impossible situation in order to force the individual to bring out his very best."[13] It is as though the unconscious purpose that is at work in Martin, and that gradually becomes more and more visible as these dreams progress, is seeking the best in him. He must now exchange the good for the best, always a difficult choice. If we are in a bad place, feeling miserable, with the evidence all around us that where we are is an undesirable state, then we are willing to move on. But if we are in a good place and life is okay, and we have some positive things at work for us, it is difficult to give this up for the best. That is a truly hard choice to make, but it was this kind of choice that was forced upon Martin.[14]

Not long after this dream, Martin literally gave up his room in the commune. It was not that he decided on the basis of this dream, "I should give up my room." Rather, the choice made in the dream found expression instinctively in a decision on his part to leave where he was and undertake a

---

[13]C. G. Jung, The Interpretation of Visions; Spring 1962, p. 154. The quotation continues: "Otherwise one stops short of one's best, one is not complete, one does not realize oneself. What is needed is an impossible situation where one has to renounce one's own will and one's own wit and do nothing but wait and trust to the impersonal power of growth and development."

[14]Martin commented as follows on this dream: "The work on the room and the finished product was the product of the puer. It was a fanciful undertaking and the finished product had a kind of charming, fairy tale quality about it since it was so constructed in the basement of the house that when entering you had the experience of being surprised to discover a wonderful room hidden in a deep cave. So I would say that this room was the end product of 'good' puer energies. To me it kind of marked the last stage in an adolescent search for identity. As you pointed out, if I were to go on with my growth I had to give this up. But to me there seems to be a paradox here since unless the adolescent puer ego had attained a strong enough sense of its identity—if there was not strength enough in the ego—then it would not have been able to give itself up to greater demands."

journey. It is a suggestion of the way the inner and outer events of our lives have a secret connection. Martin's first intent at the time he decided to leave was to travel to Germany in order to study the work of the existentialist philosopher, Martin Heidegger. Martin Heidegger is a very intellectual and heady philosopher who deals with words as though they were things-in-themselves. His philosophy is way up in the stratosphere of thought, about 30,000 feet above the earth. Martin's interest in pursuing the study of Heidegger's philosophy suggests where Martin was: way up in his head. What his unconscious thought of his choice to go to Germany and study this philosophy is clear in the dream that follows.

Dream 5

The fifth dream:

> "The motorcycle had been running well all day and I was having great fun zooming over the cobblestone streets of a small village in Germany; until I tried to take the steepest hill in the village. As I neared the top, the motorcycle conked out and began to slide backwards down the hill. I looked over my shoulder and became terrified by what I saw. Less than a half of a block below me the street abruptly broke off and below the street some 300 yards down was a lake with rough, black waters. I could do nothing; I could not stop the motorcycle from sliding. Its speed increased and I could not even manage to jump off. I was frightened for my life.
>
> "The motorcycle, with me helplessly caught on it, did not stop, but continued sliding downwards over the street's end, falling toward the rough, black waters of the lake."

The dream begins with Martin on a motorcycle. Martin wrote of this, "I clearly remember waking from the dream and immediately thinking that the motorcycle was energy within me, some sort of power within me for living and being. I am not able to say more exactly what I mean." It is interesting to observe how we get around in our dreams. Means of conveyance in dreams include driving a car, travelling by ship or train, flying airplanes, riding in a bus, bicycling, swimming, walking, running, and even flying unaided. To understand why a dream chooses a particular means of conveyance we need the dreamer's associations; the means of conveyance chosen may have a very individual reason. Nevertheless, we can hazard some conjectures about the general meaning of these various types of transportation.

A car is very close to the ego. It does what we want it to do, obeys our will, and serves us in the outer world. It often represents a certain amount of energy available to the ego to use as it goes about its tasks in life. If something happens to our car in a dream we can expect to feel it the next day. For instance, if we dream that our car will not work, it is not surprising that the next day we may not function well and may have difficulties getting around. I also find that usually when we are not driving the car, but are only riding in it while someone else drives, the dream has a way of ending badly. Something unfortunate happens all too often in such cases—an accident perhaps, or we lose the way. It is as though the car represents the energy of the ego and if someone else is driving, it suggests that we are turning our lives over to another figure within us and we are not taking charge. Car dreams seldom are profound, for cars are machines and represent a kind of mechanical functioning. We cannot expect to reach the kingdom of heaven in a car, though they are useful for everyday life.

Ships have a deeper significance. There is something numinous and archetypal about a ship. The early church called itself a ship because it took the believer across life to a safe shore on the other side. To this day, the main body of a church is called the "nave," the name coming from the part of the old galleys where the rowers used to sit. The ship seems to symbolize what carries us through life; perhaps the body, or the Self, or, since a ship is man-made, a certain set of ideas or beliefs which are working for us. So to have a good ship under you in a dream suggests something solid is taking you through life.

Airplanes, of course, go through the air. The air represents the world of spirit or intellect. We sometimes say of intellectual people, "that person lives in an ivory tower," meaning high up above the ground in an airy, mental world. We also speak of a "flight of ideas." Airplanes are also man-made, so they sometimes represent getting some place by means of ideas or concepts, for concepts also are man-made. Sometimes this is useful. Ideas can take us far and fast. On the other hand, to have ideas is not to have experiences, just as flying in a plane high above the ground gives us no experience of what is below. Since in our particular time of history people have a tendency to be too much up in the air anyway, flying in airplanes is often a dubious means of conveyance in our dreams. Naturally, this point is aggravated if the plane should crash, for the only safe plane is a plane that has a positive and healthy relationship to what is on the ground.

A bus is a public means of transportation; there is nothing individual about a bus. If we are swept along too much with collective opinions, going along through life with the crowd, this may be reflected in a dream as travelling on a bus or trolley car. On the other hand, we must remember again that this is an individual matter. For instance one woman reports that, for her, being in a bus is good because it reminds her that she is in one way "just an ordinary person." As a child she was made to feel too special, and for her this is a helpful compensation.

Bicycling is a generally positive means of transportation in a dream because it is so individual, and because we make it go by our own power. Bicycles also have good "soul"; they feel good to ride, and, in spite of their being man-made machines and not found in nature, they somehow feel natural because we are in contact with our environment when we ride a bicycle. People who seldom or never ride bicycles in their outer lives find they do so in their dreams. The bike moves because we drive the wheels around and around in a circular motion; it stays upright because of the gyroscopic effects of the moving wheels. Such a circular movement is characteristic of the individuation process, which moves around and around a center with a circular or spiral form of energy. The ancient alchemists called this the "circulatio."

Water is the symbol par excellence for the unconscious, so swimming suggests that someone is acquiring the ability to navigate safely through the waters of the unconscious. This is in contrast to drowning, which suggests that we are drowning in the unconscious and symbolizes a state of danger. The more we know of the inner world the better we are likely to be at swimming in our dreams. If we find we can swim under the water, as well as above the water, so much the better.

Walking or running are positive means of travel in dreams. Here we are right on the ground, and are getting around in a natural way under our own power. Running suggests good conditioning, and the energy and dedication of an athlete. Running dreams can be contrasted with dreams in which we try to move but seem rooted to the ground. In these dreams it is as though we are so unconscious we cannot get moving. It is as though the dream says we cannot make psychological progress. In running, the opposite condition prevails. We acquire a certain lightness of movement made possible by our increasing psychological awareness.

Flying through the air unaided is much more suspect. Man is made to walk on the ground, not fly through the air. Flying dreams suggest a too youthful (puer) attitude, unrealistic ideas, a person who is not "grounded." Exceptions might occur when the flight represents the equivalent of the "magical flight" of the shamans, a state resulting from unusual psychic powers.

In Martin's dream the means of conveyance is a motorcycle, which he immediately identified as a form of energy. It is like a car; mechanical and noisy. In addition, our dreamer is driving it carelessly, and the image of the motorcycle roaring up the medieval streets of a German city is an offensive picture. The motorcycle can be understood as representing a puerile form of energy, a kind of reckless, heedless masculinity. This is confirmed by the hedonist aspect of the dream—he is having "great fun," and is "zooming" over the cobblestone streets. Finally he tries to go up the highest hill in the village, an image that suggests he has fallen into what the Greeks called "hybris." Hybris is an ego inflation, an arrogance, which is always punished by the gods. When a human being gets too high up, he suffers from hybris, and the gods (the unconscious) seek to correct this inflated attitude, often by drastic means. As we will see later, hybris is a problem that Martin suffered from time and again, and it always produced a compensatory reaction from the unconscious.

So Martin's attitude is wrong, and the unconscious seeks to compensate and correct it. Suddenly the motorcycle's power is cut off and the machine begins to roll backwards down the hill. Martin is helpless; his sense of power is gone, and he panics. Earlier I suggested that dreams can be regarded as sent from God. On the psychological level, this means that dreams originate from our inner center or Self, which is the self-regulating and guiding function of the psyche. An experience with the Self is like an experience with God. Experientially the two are indistinguishable, and the Self, while it cannot be said to be identical with the Transcendent Deity, does seem to be, as Jung once put it, "a vessel for divine grace."[15] But most of us are used to thinking of God as loving, beneficent, and kind. Can such a dark and threatening dream as this also be said to come from God?

Of course, for one of the main functions of God is to cut us off from a wrong path. This usually requires drastic action on God's part. Dark and frightening dreams are the dark, threatening side of God, that side of God that is constellated when man goes against the purpose for which God has created him. Even the nightmare can be ascribed to divine activity, as the Bible says through the words of Job:

---

[15]C. G. Jung, *Letters Vol. I*, p. 349; Bollingen Series, Princeton University Press, 1973.

"If I say, 'My bed will comfort me, my couch will soothe my pain, you frighten me with dreams and terrify me with visions.' "[16] And Elihu also says, "God speaks first in one way, and then in another, but no one notices. He speaks by dreams, and visions that come in the night, when slumber comes on mankind, and men are all asleep in bed. Then it is he whispers in the ear of man, or may frighten him with fearful sights, to turn him away from evil-doing, and make an end of his pride; to save his soul from the pit and his life from the pathway to Sheol."[17]

A good example of this side of God is found in the 22nd Chapter of Numbers, the story of Balaam, his donkey, and the angel of Yahweh.[18] In this tale, the prophet Balaam has been approached by the Moabite king, Balak, who wants Balaam to come and prophesy for him about the Hebrews; he is afraid of them and they are on the point of invading his land. Balaam has agreed to go and is journeying to Moab on his donkey when the animal inexplicably turns off the road and goes into the field. Balaam angrily beats her back onto the road, but a little later, when they come to a narrow path between some vineyards, the donkey halts and presses against the wall, hurting Balaam's foot. Furious, Balaam again beats the donkey forward. But now the donkey suddenly lies down on the ground under Balaam, and this time he is livid with anger and shouts to the donkey, "You have made sport of me. I wish I had a sword in my hand, for then I would kill you." Then it was that Balaam's eyes were opened and he saw why the donkey was behaving so strangely: right there in his path was the angel of Yahweh with a drawn sword in his hand. The angel declared, "Behold, I have come forth to withstand you, because your way is perverse before me; and the ass saw me, and turned aside from me these three times. If she had not turned aside from

---

[16]Job 7:13-14.
[17]Job 33:14-18.
[18]For a fine analysis of this story see Rivkah Sharf Kluger's book *Satan in the Old Testament*.

me, surely just now I would have slain you and let her live."[19]

We learn from the angel of Yahweh that he comes because God is angry that Balaam would go to Balak and prophesy for him. "God's anger was kindled because he went; and the angel of the Lord took his stand in the way as his adversary."[20] The word "adversary" is, in Hebrew, the word "satan." "Satan," in its verbal form, means "to hinder free forward movement as by fettering a person." In Greek the word corresponding to satan is *Diabolos*, translated "devil" in English, which means "to throw something across one's path." Long before satan was differentiated from God and made into a metaphysical being, God Himself was thought to have a satan side, that is, a side to Himself that would stand across man's path to block his way and be an adversary to him.

As the story continues, Balaam and the angel of the Lord get into a confrontation, and as a result of this Balaam becomes aware of God's Will for him: he is to go on to Moab and prophesy for Balak, but is only to utter exactly what Yahweh tells him to utter. Now Balaam is allowed to continue on his way, but as a result of the encounter with the angel of God, who was a "satan" to him, Balaam is aware of the Divine Will.

Psychologically, this story is a personification of what can be called the dark side of the Self. There is something that confronts us as an adversary and blocks our way. This dark reality appears at precisely those moments when we are straying from the path that is intended for us, and when our egocentricity must be countered by the larger Will within us if our life is not to miss the mark.

The dark side of the Self may be constellated outside of us or inside of us. An outer event may stand in our way and block our path, perhaps in the form of a broken relationship, or an unexpected turn of events. Or it may be an inner

---

[19]Numbers 22:29, 32-33, RSV.
[20]Numbers 22:22 RSV.

confrontation in the form of a neurosis, a compulsion, or an over-whelming anxiety. Such confrontations can be frightening and destructive if we do not become conscious of the meaning of the situation; we must remember that the angel of Yahweh said he would have killed Balaam if Balaam had not seen him in time.

Fortunately, there are usually warnings prior to such a dark confrontation, and these warnings are frequently expressed in dreams. This is one of their helpful functions. But if we do not heed such warnings, unpleasant things may happen: the unraveling of our personality, an unfortunate accident, or perhaps an illness.

Martin's dream of the motorcycle plunging down the hill falls into this type of experience. An "angel of Yahweh" has sent this dream, which stands across his path and blocks the way because Martin is going in the wrong direction, both literally and psychologically. Fortunately for Martin he heeded the warning, turned aside from his intention to go to Germany, and made other plans. That the dream is only a warning, and the matter is not yet determined, is represented in the dream by the fact that Martin does not actually fall into the lake, but is only plunging toward it. This tells us that there is still the possibility of a change, for Martin has not yet had an irrevocable fall into the black and stormy waters below him.

The black and stormy waters are an important detail of the dream. They symbolize the "anger" of the unconscious, and remind us of the fairy tale of the Fisherman and His Wife (one of Grimms' collection). In this story a humble fisherman who lives with his wife in a pigsty, catches a flounder that turns out to be an enchanted prince. The flounder explains this to the fisherman and asks to be thrown back, and the kind fisherman graciously obliges, goes home, and tells his wife what happened. His wife is terribly angry, and chastizes her husband for having thrown the fish back without having asked a wish. At his wife's insistence the fisherman goes back, recalls the flounder from the sea, and asks that instead of the pigsty in which they live they might have a little cottage. The wish is granted, but this does not satisfy his wife who continually asks for more and more: a castle, to be the king in a palace, to be emperor, even to be pope. Each time the fisherman returns to ask another wish the sea is stormier and blacker than before. Finally the fisherman's wife demands that she become like God Himself, but at this the flounder becomes furiously angry. The story tells us that "a great storm was raging, and blowing so hard that the fisherman could scarcely keep his feet . . . and the sea came in with black waves as high as church-towers and mountains."[21] Then the flounder commands that everything be taken away, and the fisherman and his wife are returned to the miserable pigsty from which they began. Clearly the stormy, black sea represents the anger of the unconscious at the weak fisherman and his demanding wife.

In the same way the blackness and disturbance of the lake in Martin's dream can be understood as the "anger" of the unconscious, and had he fallen into the lake it would have represented a dangerous psychological state, which might have been experienced on the conscious level as profound confusion, anxiety, depression, or, in a person subject to it, even psychosis. Martin can be grateful that the dream stopped short of this plunge into the dark waters below.

This is the only dream in the series upon which Martin directly acted. Though he did not exactly interpret the dream as we have done here, he did decide on the basis of this dream not to go to Germany. This decision put him on his right path again. Instead of the trip to Germany to study the philosophy of Heidegger, he set out for California to visit a friend in Berkeley. As we might have suspected from his third dream, Martin hitchhiked across the country. Dreams two and three in the series were now literally coming about.

---

[21]*Grimm's Fairy Tales*, Pantheon Books, a Division of Random House, New York, 1944; p. 111.

Dream 6

Martin arrived safely in California and found his friend
in Berkeley. That was as far as his conscious plans had gone,
but the unconscious had further plans for him. After visiting
in Berkeley two weeks he realized he could not stay longer
with his friend, and yet he had nowhere else to go. Again
we may imagine what great anxiety his parents must have
been experiencing all of this time. As mentioned earlier, his
father in particular may have feared that his son would turn
out to be a failure, and perhaps was saying to himself that
his dropping out of school and "bumming around the country" were the inevitable result of his taking up with the
"communists" in the commune. No one could have guessed
that all of this time a secret purpose was at work. At this
point Martin remembered that he had once heard of a certain monastery in the Southwest, and he set out to find it,
travelling as before by the power of his thumb.

It was a long way from Berkeley to the Southwest, but
he made the journey successfully. The last sixteen miles
were along a remote, unpaved road. There was no traffic and
Martin had to walk, but he related that this was an almost
ecstatic experience for him, and that he felt a great joy and
vigor as he walked those last miles through the desert to the
monastery. It was now midwinter, and the desert must have
been cool and beautiful. He was now in exactly the kind of
country described in his second dream. At last he arrived,
unannounced of course, at the door of the monastery. The
surprised monks must have been very kind. They took him
in without too many questions, gave him a cell of his own,
the run of the monastery, and welcomed him into their life.
It was on the third day of his stay in the monastery that
Martin had his sixth dream:

"While I am asleep on the hard straw bed in the
monks' cell my heart begins to beat wildly. I remain half
asleep—half awake. It is as if I am too frightened to
allow myself to awaken completely for fear that I am
dying and that, if awake, the pain will be too great to
bear.

"My heart continues to beat wildly for a few more minutes. Then, gradually it begins to slow down and at last it stops altogether. Death.

"Then there is a wonderful stirring inside of me, and I feel my spent heart being replaced by one much larger and much stronger. And, as the new life from the heart begins to fill my veins, I am told that this heart was my mother's."

This is clearly a healing dream. The situation Martin finds himself in is reminiscent of the cult of Asklepius, ancient Greek god of healing.[22] In ancient Greece, if you desired a healing from the god who was the source of all health, you might undertake a journey to one of his sacred shrines. Once at the temple of the god the priests would interview you to be sure you had been appropriately invited by the god; such an invitation might have been given to you through a dream. Rites of confession and purification would follow, and then you would be led into an inner chamber of the temple known as the *abaton* (which means "a place not to be entered into uninvited"), and here you would await the presence of the god who would come in a healing dream.

The journey to the temple of the god amounted to a pilgrimage; that is, a journey undertaken for a sacred purpose. Martin has, unwittingly, made such a journey. He has come from the Midwest to the faraway Southwest and has unconsciously been led to what is as close to a healing shrine as we have in our culture. His monk's cell can be likened to the inner chamber of the Asklepian Temple, and his long journey and sixteen mile walk to the monastery, to a ritual of purification. In fact, Martin even recalls throwing away his cigarettes as he walked along! The healing dream of the renewed heart has archetypal roots that go deeply into the human psyche.

In spiritual or psychological healing a pilgrimage is always essential. No one ever becomes whole if they sit and wait for healing to come to them. In some way a journey

---

[22]See my book *Healing and Wholeness*; New York: The Paulist Press, 1977, Chapter III.

must be undertaken, even if it is just the journey to the office of the priest or psychotherapist. Parish priests often get requests from a family member to go and visit so-and-so who is having a problem. However, such visits seldom do any good, and often have negative results, for if a person wants to become well or wants to overcome a problem, he cannot wait for help to come to him, but must be willing to undertake a pilgrimage to search for it himself.

This dream also shows us the intent of the unconscious: to bring about that fundamental change in personality that is best represented in the image of death and renewal. To die and be born again is an appropriate archetypal symbol for the renewal of life. It is the central symbol of Christianity; the Christian dies with Christ at his baptism, and then is resurrected with him to a new life. Among the shamans also this was a central symbol, for shamans were called to their healing vocations through an initiatory illness or crisis in which the shaman experienced himself as being dismembered and dying, and then being gathered together and brought back to life again.[23]

The renewal comes about through gaining a new heart. We have seen that in going to Germany Martin was acting from his head, and he intended to pursue still more matters of the head through studying existentialist philosophy. His dream indicates this is not where Martin's development lies; not the head, but the heart is the source of new life for him. His old heart must die, and a new heart waits to take its place.

The heart is a symbol for the feeling function, emotional life, for love, and for courage. We speak of a "broken heart" to signify a state of grief, or a "bleeding heart" to suggest intense love for someone. A beloved is called a "sweetheart," and when we have compassion for someone we say our heart goes out to that person. The Bible uses the word "heart" hundreds of times, always as a synonym for the inner man and his emotional life, and the American

---

[23]ibid. Chapter IV, and cf. Mircea Eliade's *Shamanism*, Princeton University Press, 1964.

Indians spoke of people as having either a "good heart" or a "bad heart." Of a man who lost courage they would say that his "heart left him," just as we would say that a person becomes "disheartened." On the other hand, to have enthusiasm and courage is to have a "high heart" and to be a "hearty person."

Emotional life, for a man, always is close to the feminine. Emotions lead to woman, to mother or sweetheart, for a woman always stands on the side of a man's heart. This is a dangerous, but life-giving area for a man. Many a man who is too close to his mother for comfort, takes refuge from her in some area where she cannot follow. Often it is the intellectual world, a realm into which he can escape where the dangerous feminine influence cannot pursue him; such was probably the case with Martin. But as soon as a man comes down to earth, there is mother and the world of emotion waiting for him. And so it should be, for only if he comes to terms with matters of the heart does a man truly become himself.

In the dream, the new heart Martin receives is his "mother's heart." There may be three different ways in which Martin gets a renewed heart from his "mother": through his personal mother, through Mother Church, and through the archetypal Great Mother. We have already made the acquaintance of Martin's father, now it is time to meet his mother. Of her Martin wrote,

"My relationship with my mother is a good one. I love her very much and of course she loves me very much as well. Yet I am not close to my mother the way some children are close to their mothers. By this I mean that I have never been one to confide in my mother. Never while I was growing up did I tell my mother what I was thinking or what I was doing unless for some reason she demanded to know. What she knows of my growing up she knows from her watching and intuiting.

"My mother is a good woman with a strong, simple religious faith. She is a Catholic as is my father. Both of them are cradle Catholics, but my mother's faith is the living one. She is gifted with children. She is a first grade teacher

now and has, off and on during her married life, taught the
first years of primary school. My mother is not especially
gifted in any other way. She is of average intelligence and
without any educated interest in artistic things or intellectual questions. She has no talent in something like
music or painting, but she can sew very well. She makes a
very pleasant house and likes doing this very much. She is
not a particularly strong person in her convictions, though
she is by no means weak, and often enough I have the feeling that she is not able to or does not want to admit there is
real evil all about us and even in us. I think that for this
reason she is not so gifted with the children once they become adolescents. She begins to lose hold. Her faith is a
source of much strength to her although at times she becomes pious in the expression of her faith. My mother is a
generous, energetic, and giving person—more than most
women. I remember my father often saying that my mother
was one of those people who had a *'big heart'"* (italics mine).

Martin praises his mother as a good woman who makes
a good house, but do we detect in what he says a hidden
tendency to depreciate her? Does he see her virtues as
slightly inferior and her deficiences as more serious than
they are? Martin says that she is not gifted in any other way
than working with small children. Why can't he just say that
she is gifted in working with small children? He points out
that she has no interest in artistic things or intellectual questions, no talent in something like music or painting. Why
does he point that out unless he has some standard in his
mind that says *these* are the things that are really important?
It is possible that Martin is evaluating his mother from some
lofty masculine perch, which unconsciously puts down her
instinctive feminine side, and has a devaluating attitude
toward his mother's feminine strengths. The fact is, Martin
evidently had an earth mother, a rare and great gift to a man.
She was evidently a woman who was comfortable with her
femininity, and who was probably much shrewder than
Martin imagined, though her intelligence went into human
relationships rather than into lofty intellectual matters. Such
a depreciating attitude toward the feminine probably would

be a characteristic of a person who pursued existentialist philosophy too one-sidedly.

Whether or not Martin has a depreciating attitude toward the feminine, the fact is that the new source of life for him comes from the feminine, from the heart of his mother. This may refer to his own mother and her positive influence upon him; a man or woman who has had the gift of a nourishing, loving relationship with his mother in early years acquires an underlying strength and sense of security that comes to his aid again and again in life. This is true especially in times of crisis, provided that he or she has overcome the childishness that is also often a lingering effect of the positive mother; a child with such a positive mother often hates to leave her and the charmed and secure world she has provided. So when the dream says that the new heart came from his mother we can understand this as a gift to Martin from his personal mother, as well as a symbol for the infusion of new life from the feminine qualities within him that the word "mother" represents.

But there is also the matter of Mother Church, for at the time of this dream Martin is in the lap of Mother Church. Statues of the Holy Mother Mary must have been here and there in the monastery and these must have been a nurturing mother to the monks and their guests. By returning to the womb of Mother Church, Martin is placed in touch with life-giving feminine symbols and images, and with the world of the irrational that the Roman Catholic Church has succeeded in maintaining and keeping available for the faithful through its symbols and sacraments.

But behind the power of Mother Church is the archetypal or Great Mother. The unconscious is the mother of us all. Every one of us has two mothers: a personal, biological mother out of whom we emerged literally and physically, and a spiritual, psychological mother in the matrix of the collective unconscious out of which the ego emerges, even as life once emerged out of the depths of the great ocean. A living contact with the collective unconscious can put us in touch with a world of life-giving images and archetypal symbols that can connect us with energy. We do not reach this inner world through our heads, but through our hearts; that is, through pain, suffering, emotion, love, caring. Through his long pilgrimage, his attention to his dreams, and his immersion in the monastery, Martin has succeeded in contacting this inner realm of eternal and timeless images, the world of the Great Mother out of whom rebirth emerges.

With such a beautiful and impressive dream one would think that Martin had "arrived," especially that he would be grateful to the realm of the feminine for renewing his life, and humble that he had been given the gift of new life. But egocentricity is hard to overcome, and it takes many impressions before deep truths sink into our being in such a way as to eradicate our false attitudes and shallow philosophies. So once again Martin has to undergo a fall, which happens in his next dream.

Martin also commented that further dreams were necessary in order to complete this stage of his development, because he still had an unresolved religious problem. He had, he relates, cast aside the religion of his childhood, yet was driven from within to come to terms with his Catholic tradition, and had a great urge to find out what religion, and Christianity in particular, was all about. "It was," he relates, "the only thing which interested me at that time." As moving as the dream of the mother's heart was, Martin still did not have answers to the questions which were pressing upon him, so it is not surprising that this series of dreams does not end here but goes on to a still more dramatic conclusion.

Dream 7

About midway through his stay at the monastery, several weeks after the dream of the new heart, Martin dreams as follows:

"The cliffs are high and fall off, straight down, an unknown distance. I have been told often of their danger. All of the people who live in the country around the cliffs know how dangerous the cliffs are, and only a

few, the most courageous and the most foolish, have
dared to climb them. Even the Indians of old who once
lived in the country around the cliffs, as the legend goes,
showed fear when they talked of them. But, it is said,
they seldom talked of them.

"I was going to climb them. I took no heed of the
warnings of the people. When I reached the top of the
cliffs with little trouble I thought that all of the people
and the Indians of old were mistaken. I felt proud, and
from the top of the cliffs I sneered at all who lived below
and had not dared the climb, calling them timid grandmothers.

"I went on walking along the edge at the top of the
cliffs, peering over into the abyss. Suddenly, the edge
cracked and I fell into the abyss. The unbearable speed
and twisting of the fall caused my body to be changed
into a weed. When after hours of falling I hit the bottom
of the abyss I, the weed, began to burn with flames that
shot up to the edge of the cliffs, to the very edge where
my fall had begun. I burned and burned until I, the
weed, had become ashes covering the bottom of the
abyss.

"Then from a deep, hidden place that was even
below the bottom of the abyss, a great but gentle voice
came forth, pleading, 'Jesus, Jesus, Jesus', and with the
sound of the voice I was resurrected."

Our egocentricity dies a hard death.[24] One would think
that after the previous dream Martin would have found a
new humility, but whatever changes the dream of the new
heart brought to him, they had not yet become permanent.
Of course, the very beauty and power of that dream was
likely to bring about the danger of hybris, for it is a fact that
when someone touches something of the spirit, at that very
moment there is the immediate danger of misusing it and

---

[24]For a more complete analysis of egocentricity see my book *The Man Who Wres-
tled with God*, published by the Religious Publishing Company, 198 Allendale
Road, King of Prussia, Pa. 19406; pp. 25-26.

becoming arrogant. Evidently something like this happened with Martin; at least the problem of hybris remained in him, and so this dream takes the matter up again.

The question of the correct attitude we should have to ourselves is not easy. Jesus once declared, "Anyone who loses his life . . . will find it."[25] Sometimes this has been construed to mean that one should not have much of an ego, that the ego should stand aside and become as nothing so God's Will can operate. On the other hand, it is not possible to give up what we do not have. God cannot use our ego for His Will if there is not an ego there to be used. From the psychological point of view, it is extremely important for a strong ego to be established; only a strong ego can withstand the pressures of the individuation process. However, if wholeness is to be reached, sooner or later the ego must be subordinated to the Self, which is, on the level of psychological experience, the Will of God.

So there is the constant danger of the ego's having too little sense of its own power and importance or too much. In the former case, one suffers from crippling inferiority feelings which make one too weak and ineffective to be an instrument for the Self. On the other hand, to be filled with too great an idea of one's own power is to run into the danger of hybris. The answer is "modesty," a word that means to take correct measure of oneself. To be modest is to see ourselves as we are, with neither too small nor too large an opinion of our abilities, thus to have an estimate of ourselves that fits what we are. The Chinese wisdom book, the I Ching, says of the hexagram "Modesty " "Thus the superior man reduces that which is too much and augments that which is too little. He weighs things and makes them equal."[26]

Clearly this dream shows that Martin has not yet achieved the correct attitude of modesty, but falls again into hybris, which the dream tries to compensate with the plunge into the abyss. His arrogance is enflamed by his

[25]Matt. 10:39.
[26]Richard Wilhelm translation, Bollingen Foundation, Pantheon Books, 1950, p. 67. Hexagram 15 is the only hexagram without any unfavorable lines.

successful climb up the steep and dangerous cliffs, a climb that he performs easily. This climb can be likened to a spiritual ascent, up to a high place where one can see a long distance all around. The fact that Martin did succeed in climbing the cliffs easily, suggests that he does in fact have considerable spiritual power. He is a gifted person and is able to make such steep ascents with relative ease; he has the gifts to raise himself above the level of consciousness of the general strata of mankind. His modesty will include a proper recognition of these gifts, not a false humility that denies that life has endowed him with any special insights or powers. One cannot attain wholeness by denying special gifts or abilities that have been given to us, as Jesus indicated in his Parable of the Talents.[27]

But once having scaled the cliffs Martin immediately succumbs to the deadly hybris. He stands at the top of the cliffs and feels proud, and even sneers at those who remained below. Then comes a surprising comment, for we are told that he mocked the people below, calling them "timid grandmothers."

This expression, "timid grandmothers," casts aspersions upon the feminine principle. It looks as though Martin, having scaled those masculine spiritual heights, has fallen back again into his devaluation of the feminine. Yet it was exactly the power of the feminine, represented by the heart of his mother, that rescued and renewed him in the previous dream. This rejection and diminution of the feminine is too much; something must be done to correct once and for all this masculine arrogance, and the dream goes on to provide the necessary correction.

Suddenly the edge of the cliff cracks, the ground gives way underneath him, and Martin plunges down, down, down into the abyss below. The abyss is the world of the Mothers. The feminine world he so despised rushes up now to meet him and he himself becomes like a weed and begins to burn. Martin related that at the time of this dream he had been reading the Psalms and the image of the weed and the

---

[27]Matt. 25:14ff.

fire made him think of certain verses which he quoted as follows:

Psalm 101: "For my days are vanishing like smoke, my bones burn away like fire, my heart is withered like the grass." (A verse which reminds us, of course, of the dream before of the new heart).

Psalm 102: "As for man, his days are like grass; he flowers like the flower of the field; the wind blows and he is gone, and his place never sees him again."[28]

These verses emphasize the transitory, finite, limited aspect of our human condition, exactly the kind of corrective to his arrogance that Martin needs.

But that is not the end of the story. God does not want to destroy us, only to purge us of that which is unworthy. Psychologically put, the unconscious does not wish to destroy the ego; a whole person is possible only when there is an ego around which the Self can rally, and through which the Self can be expressed. So Martin is not destroyed but, at the last minute, is saved again. After he is burned and burned, that is, purged of unworthy qualities, purified in the fire of the unconscious, he is then reborn.

The power that renews him to life is, perhaps, once again, the feminine power, for it may be that the voice that pleads, "Jesus, Jesus, Jesus" is the voice of the Mother of God calling upon the Saviour for intercession for a needy sinner. That is putting it in religious language. The same thing said psychologically would be that the archetypal feminine powers come forth once more and restore this needy ego to its proper relationship with the Self. With the sound of this voice, Martin is resurrected.

This part of the dream is a good example of what the church has always called "the grace of God." The grace of God is an unmerited, undeserved saving gift from on High. In psychological language, it represents the fact that the Self can and does act to rescue us in our extremity, and comes to

---

[28]*The Psalms*. A New Translation From the Hebrew Arranged For Singing To the Psalmody of Joseph Gelineau. Paulist Press Deus Books, New York, 1968.

our aid at precisely the point where we are most defeated and helpless. In one sense the emergence of wholeness is always coincident with the defeat of the ego. Only when we have come to the end of our own resources do we truly begin to feel and experience the power of God, and understand what it is that holds us up when everything else fails.

The grace of God looms large in Christian thought, but is not a part of the imagery of the East. In the East, God is not represented as interested in saving man; if man is saved it is largely through his own efforts. In the East, one attains Nirvana, union with God, through correct living, correct meditation, and correct renunciation of the world and its desires. All of this works quite objectively; it is a matter of following correct spiritual law, and the process is about as personal to us as the law of gravity. Which perspective is the true one? From the standpoint of the psychology of individuation, both perspectives are true, and sometimes one attitude, sometimes another attitude is most appropriate.

Joseph Campbell, in his book *Myths to Live By*, tells the story of the kitten people and the monkey people. The kitten waits mewing for its mother to come along, grab it by the back of its neck, and take it to safety. The baby monkey waits for its mother to come bounding along, then leaps on her back and hangs on for dear life. Sometimes we have to wait helplessly for the grace of God to come and rescue us; at other times we have to do our own work and hang on for dear life. If we live only by the first attitude it results in an over-dependence on God, a childishness on our part, a wanting to be taken care of, a refusal to grow up and pull our own spiritual oar in life. If we live only by the second attitude we eventually exhaust ourselves, and come to an impasse when our own resources are no longer able to help.

In this dream, Martin experiences the grace of God; he had to become like one of the kitten people and experience his own helplessness as a cure for his egocentricity. However, in the eighth and last dream of our series Martin has the opposite experience.

Dream 8

The day after the previous dream Martin dreamt as follows:

"I meet face to face a tall, strong, black clad cleric. He pokes his log-like finger at me and shouts that I was to give no ear to the voice which pleaded for Jesus the night before and that my resurrection experience was purely and simply an illusion. His words hit my face like bullets.

"I am overwhelmed and frightened by this awful message. I am silent for a few minutes while I collect myself and try to steady my shaking legs. Once calmed a bit I say to the cleric with a conviction of my whole self, 'No, you are wrong.' The cleric makes no reply. He turns and leaves me."

The dream of the fall from the cliff had a profound effect upon Martin. It was as though this series of dreams began to have a cumulative effect upon his consciousness. In the words of Cathy in *Wuthering Heights* that we mentioned earlier, they were altering the color of his mind. An appreciation of the significance of irrational but highly meaningful forces at work in his life, manifested through his dreams, was becoming a part of Martin's conscious personality, with a resulting reorientation of his life around a new Center, and, as a consequence, the formation of a truly religious attitude. At just this crucial moment, when some permanent changes are beginning to take place in Martin, comes this dream in which a black clad priest tries to persuade him that the experience he had in his dream the night before was purely an illusion.

The black clad priest can be identified as the devil. That is, psychologically this cleric plays one of the archetypal roles that the devil has always played in Christian lore. In Christian imagery, the devil appears either as a personification of what has been repressed and is now seeking to return, or as a personification of certain psychological qualities that have gained dominance over consciousness and so are serving an evil purpose by excluding the whole. The devil, for instance, has horns, which he got from Dionysus, or from the horned god who was worshiped in ancient witchcraft. He also is shown with a goat's foot, a legacy from Pan, the nature god of Greece. Sometimes he appears in the form of a beautiful, seductive woman, a personification of the qualities of Aphrodite that were rejected by the Christian Church. Dionysus, Pan, Aphrodite, are gods who were rejected by Christianity; that is, personifications of archetypal life patterns were repressed by the church, and so appear devilish when they seek to return.

But there are also certain psychological qualities that have become the dominant qualities of a particular culture to the exclusion of the rest of the psyche. This too appears as evil because this exclusion denies the whole man. In our culture the rationalistic, materialistic attitude performs this function. We have gone too far in this direction, and, as a result, have denied that which is irrational, symbolic, and feminine in favor of that which is rational, logical, and masculine. As we have seen, Martin had been very much under the domination of this rationalistic attitude. Under the influence of his dreams this rationalistic attitude has to give way. But it dies a hard death. At the very moment when a fundamental change might take place the rationalistic attitude comes back in the form of the priest.

We should not be surprised that the dream chose the black clad cleric to personify the devil. In times past, the devil frequently chose to appear as a priest. In medieval lore it was one of the favorite forms the devil took. Indeed, he particularly liked it if he could find his way in this guise into a pulpit and preach. In addition, Martin associated the priest in the dream with a particular Jesuit of his acquaintance who was, in fact, a highly rationalistic person who would have decried anything as irrational as dreams. In this way the dream suggests that the devil, that is, an overvaluation of the intellect versus feeling, rationalism versus symbolic thinking, the mind versus the soul, had succeeded in getting a firm foothold in the church itself, as well as in Martin's psychology.

It is not unusual for the dark powers to rise up at exactly the moment when something important in our development might be accomplished, and try to take it away. At precisely the moment when a person might become well, the sickness often tries to reappear. In the resulting crisis, what was gained can be lost, or, if a victory can be wrested from the forces of darkness at this critical time, a permanent change can occur. In this dream, the black clad cleric performs the function of trying to take away from Martin a significant advance in consciousness by persuading him that he should give no ear to the voice that had pleaded for Jesus, and that he should regard his resurrection as an illusion. The fact that the cleric's words hit Martin like bullets emphasizes their rationalistic character, bullets in dreams often representing thoughts that have taken a rational form.

Martin is shaken by this "awful message." In the previous dream, when he was in dire straits, falling helplessly into the abyss, unseen forces came to his rescue. In this dream, no such divine help appears. Apparently it is entirely up to Martin to decide what to do. The dream suggests that if he had, through weakness or doubt or a secret alliance with evil, given in to these devilish thoughts, all would have been lost. The whole development of the last eight months would then have gone down the drain and he would have been exactly as he was before.

The situation reminds us of the story in three of the Gospels in which the rich young man comes to Jesus and asks what he must do to inherit eternal life.[29] Jesus tells him he must follow the commandments, and the young man says he has already done this. Then Jesus, perceiving that there is an urge in this rich young man to go the whole way, says to him, "Sell all that you own. . . . then come, follow me." We are told that the young man went away sorrowful, for he had many possessions. What is *not* said is perhaps the most significant part of the story. We do *not* read that Jesus ran down the street after him trying to persuade him to change his mind.

---

[29]Matt. 19:16-22; Mark 10:17-22; Luke 18:18-23. The quotation that follows is from Luke.

In certain crucial matters we are evidently given a certain power of choice, and how we exercise this power of choice is of crucial consequence to the outcome of our lives. God evidently does not interfere with this power of choice. If we make the wrong choice He does not run down the street after us to persuade us to change our minds, nor does He try to argue us into the correct choice. He does, however, give us enlightenment and guidance in making choices, even as the rich young man was led to Jesus, and Martin had his guiding dreams. But in the final analysis the choice is always ours, as Dorothy Phillips tells us in her fine book by that title.[30]

So Martin is confronted with a fateful choice. It requires all of his strength to choose as he does, for the black clad cleric, as we have seen, personifies the ruling spirit of the age, and it is an exceedingly difficult matter for an individual human being to go against the collective psychology of the age in which he lives. However, the very difficulty of affirming what he knows in the face of this collective spirit of rational negation, this "everything is nothing but" voice that robs the soul, forces Martin to become more certain of the ground on which he stands. In this way, even the devil serves the forces of inner development by making it essential for us to become conscious as the only way to withstand him. Finally, speaking with firm inner conviction, Martin is able to say, "No, you are wrong." With this the cleric simply turns and leaves him, even as satan left Jesus in the story of the Temptations in the Wilderness after Jesus became fully aware of his tempting voice, and rejected the temptations offered to him.

With this our series of dreams comes to an end. No doubt Martin continued to dream, but the unusually dramatic dreams that virtually demanded to be written down ceased for the time being. As a result of his experiences Martin was radically changed. His religious feeling and orientation returned. He was able to find a spiritual home in

---

[30]*The Choice is Always Ours, An Anthology on the Religious Way*, edited by Dorothy B. Phillips; Harper and Row Publishers, 1948, revised and enlarged in 1960.

his church and became once more a practicing Roman Catholic. He returned to school and finished his studies, married, and for several years after graduation taught in a Roman Catholic mission school overseas. He has now returned to this country and, with his wife and family, is continuing his life and studies in a fruitful way. The changes in him that his dreams helped bring about have proved to be lasting, and he tells me that he continues to record and study his dreams. No doubt they are leading him on into still more consciousness, for inner development never ceases, and the unconscious always formulates new possibilities.

MARIE'S DREAMS

The next series of dreams came to a woman around forty years of age whom we shall call Marie. Like Martin, Marie was not in therapy at the time the dreams occurred, nor were the dreams ever analyzed. The five dreams in this series came to Marie during a two week period and she recorded them because of their unusual intensity; remembering dreams had not been part of her life before this.

Marie came to see me in the spring for a single consultation because she wanted to return to school, but knew this would bring conflict with her husband. She had been married for many years, had no children, and described her relationship with her husband as like that of a brother and sister, rather than husband and wife. Her husband had, at one time, seemed to have a promising business career ahead of him, but this never developed; instead he had chosen secure but dull and mediocre work. Some months before Marie's visit to me, he had developed symptoms of a chronic illness of the sort that would increasingly incapacitate him. He had always wanted his wife around the house and now wanted her by his side more than ever to keep him company and fulfil the many needs his illness brought upon him. Marie had been a dutiful wife, and her life for all these years had consisted of routine duties and pleasures, but in spite of the confining nature of her life she remained remarkably cheerful and had a lively sense of humor.

Marie fulfilled her responsibilities to her husband out of a strong sense of Christian duty rather than out of love. Sometimes she liked her husband well enough, sometimes

125

she became irritated at him, but always she obeyed the voice within her that said she must be a dutiful wife. As one might imagine, the sexual side of their marriage was not very exciting, but there had been no extra-marital excursions on the part of either of them.

Marie had married her husband shortly before graduating from college. For the sake of her marriage she had given up plans to go on for a graduate degree that would enable her to become an educational specialist. She related that when she married she was attracted to her husband partly because of his many talents, but was disappointed when he gave them up for his more mundane work. However, her love went to a certain professor at the college who was about ten years her senior, and not to her husband. Being very shy, she had not approached the professor with her feelings. Although she did reach a friendly, first-name relationship with him, the true depth of her love for him was known only to her. For her, he was an unattainable goal, and she settled instead for her marriage. Perhaps her unusual sense of duty toward her husband was to compensate for the fact that, in her heart, she knew she had married a man whom she did not love.

During the years of her marriage, Marie had remained in love with this professor. That is to say, he remained a fantasy figure for her, and her sexual-erotic feelings centered around him. In the way women sometimes do, Marie had kept track of the whereabouts of this professor, occasionally exchanging notes, and knew that he was still teaching at the same university and, remarkably enough, had not married.

Marie was now feeling great inner pressure to return to school and complete her studies for her credentials. She was at the time of life when such unpursued goals and unlived yearnings come back with a vengeance, clamoring for fulfillment before it is too late. As long as we are in our twenties, or even thirties, there is always "the future," but when we are forty it is now or never. So the unfulfilled part of her life was vigorously rattling the bars of the cage into which it had been put, and in the process was causing considerable conflict with Marie's duty-bound conscience that declared she dare not stray from her husband or create dissension. Of course there was also the added enticement and anxiety over the fact that a return to school would mean she would again come into association with her professor, who taught in the very program she wished to enter. This seemed to her entirely wrong and sinful, an indulgence in her adulterous fantasies that had been tolerable to her Christian conscience only because they had been ascetically denied any actual fulfillment. A return to school and the professor amounted, in her timid and sensitive mind, to practically living in adultery, a delicious thought that evoked great conflict.

It was because of all this that she had come to me. After the situation had been aired and discussed I declared, in a most directive way, that I thought she should immediately make plans for a return to school. Fortunately for my clients, I seldom am as directive as this, and as a rule I refrain from giving advice; when I do the advice is practically never followed. But in this case Marie took my admonition seriously, promptly applied for admission to the school, and was soon enrolled for the following September.

For a year and a half she pursued her studies, resumed her student-teacher relationship with the professor, and bravely endured the quarrels and conflicts with her husband that she had known her return to school would evoke. Then, about halfway through her graduate work, the series of dreams we shall consider came to her. For some time she did nothing with these dreams, but after several months she came to see me again to report on what had happened to her since our first visit. At the end of our hour together she said rather casually that she had remembered some unusual dreams, and would like to leave a copy of them with me.

Marie has given me permission to use these dreams. We have not analyzed them because, although she was greatly impressed by them, she preferred to hold them off at a distance. In fact, in recording the dreams she has even used the third person singular, rather than the first person singular, as though they had happened to someone else. The dreams are valuable for the purposes of teaching because they represent in a capsulized way what a process of individuation might be like. Also, since Marie was not in therapy, there can be no possibility that they were influenced by a therapist or the therapeutic process. They are a pure and spontaneous product of her unconscious. However, there is the difficulty that we do not have Marie's associations to them except for a few questions I was able to ask her about them later.

Normally we would want to have the dreamer tell us what the different aspects of the dreams suggest. In this way our interpretations would be enriched and the danger of a misinterpretation would be less. These associations we lack, but on the other hand we do have a complete series of five dreams. When dreams are taken in a series, interpretation is made easier because the interpretation of one dream is aided by the others. To have only one dream to study is like coming into the middle of a movie and trying to figure out what is going on. But if you stay and watch the film long enough you can begin to fit the pieces together. So we will have to let the fact that these dreams form a relatively complete series balance our lack of personal associations.

As we will see, we cannot assume that Marie has accomplished the tasks these dreams present. They are like an invitation to her from the unconscious to participate in the great work of becoming whole, but she had not yet undergone this process. As mentioned before, some dreams seem to show us what is now happening, and other dreams show us what is a possibility for us. These dreams fall into the latter category.

Dream 1

The first of her dreams was as follows:

> "The dreamer was suffering shame from a disfigurement that covered almost the entire right side of her face. She was wearing a turban with a drape that covered it. She was walking with an older man in a heavily

populated area. He asked her to remove the drape from her face, that she had to let people see her sometime and it had best be him first. Because the dreamer had a strong emotional feeling for this man she removed the covering from her face. The feeling of shame was overwhelming. When she was able to look at him he was looking kindly at her and said, 'It's not as bad as you think,' and put his arms around her. None of the many passersby even noticed them."

This dream was highly emotional for Marie. When she woke from it she was filled with the feeling of pain and shame that the dream expressed, and also with a great love and gratitude to the man in the dream who encouraged and supported her. Who is this man? Naturally we think of the professor, and, in fact, Marie told me later that the man in the dream was like the professor, which helps us understand the dream.

Marie's face is also an important part of this dream. The face is the part of us that meets the world. We "put on a good face," and we have to go out and "face people." It is as though our soul peers out through our face, so that our face most expresses what is within us, but it also provides the soul with a shield and covering. The shame that the dreamer feels, and the disfigurement that covers the right side of her face, suggests that Marie is ashamed of her own feelings; she is not at home with her own soul and its emotions.

It is a fact that the skin, and especially the skin on our face, is extremely susceptible to emotion. If we are in love, for instance, and the person whom we love is mentioned, we may involuntarily blush. Our face suddenly glows with an embarassing redness that reveals our hidden, shy thoughts and feelings. Skin diseases are for this reason often psychogenic. I recall one young woman in her early twenties who came to me because of a bad case of acne. Her entire face was covered with virulent, ugly blotches. Her doctor had told her that while he could treat the symptoms, the cause was in herself, and this led to her visit with me. During the first consultation very little was said because the young lady could only sit and weep. Yet, within only a few weeks, her face was entirely cleared up and her skin was absolutely clear. As soon as she began to "face" certain feelings and emotions the skin ailment disappeared. It was as though her repressed emotional nature had forced its way into her consciousness by erupting in the skin condition; it was a psychological condition that she could not manage to hide any longer because it discolored her face.

In the dream, Marie tries to hide her disfigurement with the turban draped around her face. She wears a mask, an outer covering to her personality that keeps other people from seeing who she really is. Jung has called this outer mask that we put on the *persona*. It is necessary to have a persona that we can use when we do not want people to see what is going on inside of us, and an effective persona is important for ego functioning. But if we use a persona to hide our true feelings from others and ourselves because we cannot face them, the matter has gone too far. Marie can never become whole as long as she is so ashamed of her own feelings that she has to hide behind a false front.

At this point the older man appears in his helpful role and encourages Marie to remove the drape and let herself be seen, first by him. This man is a guiding and strengthening figure in the dream, a figure who leads the dreamer into the creative action of removing her mask, facing her own feelings, and letting them show. The feeling of shame that the dreamer has is so overwhelming that it amounts to a fierce resistance to removing the drape, but the emotions she feels toward this man are stronger, and because of this she does as he suggests. Obviously the emotional feeling to which the dream refers is the emotion that Marie has toward the professor. The dream is suggesting that Marie can begin to individuate through her feelings of love for this man.

Eros is like the mainspring of individuation. Because of eros, which is deep, personal love, human growth is possible. If eros is repressed, denied, or lacking, individuation does not take place. Where eros springs up it must be recognized and honored, and in the honoring of eros wholeness emerges. Until now Marie has not honored her eros, but has been ashamed of it. However, in returning to school and openly facing her emotions for the professor, Marie begins to honor her feelings, and this makes her individuation possible.

After she has removed the drape from her face, and struggled with the feeling of shame, the man looks at her kindly and gives her encouragement by placing his arms around her and saying, "It's not as bad as you think." In this way the man supports her in her time of crisis, and gives her the strength to do what must be done and endure what must be endured.

This raises the question again, "Who is this man?" To be sure, he appeared to Marie to be the professor, but in fact the actual professor had not played this role for her. He had been friendly to her after her return to school, and they had resumed their first-name relationship, but he could not have supported her as this man in the dream supported her because he knew nothing of what she felt for him. From this we must conclude that the man in the dream refers not only to the outer professor, but to an inner man as well.

The man-within-the-woman is the figure Jung calls the animus. (He is the counterpart to the woman-inside-of-the-man whom we met in Martin's first dream). The animus is a personification of the masculine qualities within a woman that, not being part of her feminine ego, have assumed the form of a masculine personality in the unconscious. As we will see a little later, this inner man can be a negative, seemingly destructive figure, but he also has his positive aspect. The positive or creative animus figure in a woman functions as her inner guide and gives great support to her ego. In this light, he appears as a life-giving figure who leads the woman into her individuation, supports her in her outer activities, and guides her through the labyrinth of her development.

As an inner figure who is an inevitable part of the psyche of every woman, the animus is an archetype, and as an archetypal figure he is numinous, that is, charged with psychic energy in such a way that his appearance evokes a

profound emotional response. As long as such an inner figure is unknown to us it is perceived outside of us in the form
of a projection. Activated figures of the unconscious project
themselves when they are not recognized by us and related
to consciously. Projection is not something we do deliberately, but something that happens to us. When not perceived as part of our inner structure, the psyche is seen
outside of us. This is the psychological basis for primitive
animism, in which the world of nature receives the projection of the unconscious, and also for the polytheistic
world of ancient peoples.

However, modern man is not without his projected
world. To be sure, we have concluded (perhaps errone-
ously!) that rocks and trees do not have spirits, so we feel
superior to primitive man inasmuch as we are free of his
unsophisticated attitude. But the net result is not necessarily
an increase in psychological consciousness, but a loss of
vitality because we now have nowhere to place the psyche;
the loss of our naive, primitive outlook has not been accompanied by a corresponding gain in self-knowledge. So projection continues to occur in modern life, but in a somewhat
more subtle form. We no longer believe in the gods and
goddesses, but we continue to make gods and goddesses of
those people who carry our projected images for us. For
instance, a figure such as the creative animus projects itself
onto a suitable man, and this man carries for a woman her
own living animus image. The same thing happens, of
course, with a man, whose anima or soul figure really projects herself onto a flesh and blood woman.

Our culture provides suitable figures for these projections in the actors and actresses of theater and entertain-
ment who, when they become sufficiently famous, are called
"stars," a word that suggests that they have caught fascinating projections from the unconscious and so have become
bigger-than-life. Any influential, unusual, or public figure

can become the recipient of the projected images of the unconscious, and that person will then carry for us something godlike. Usually when people carry projections of this sort they do not realize what is happening to them and they become inflated as a result of it. They then lose their sense of their own common humanity and limitations, and have an exaggerated idea of their importance; it is an unconscious identification with the archetypes, which works to their detriment because it robs them of their humanity and keeps them from self-knowledge.

When these projections occur in our personal relationships they become greatly complicated, for we then either overvalue or undervalue the person who carries the projected image. When this happens our husband or wife, son or daughter, lover or companion, doctor or therapist, is seen in an exaggerated light. Overvaluation occurs when the projected image is positive; undervaluation when it is a negative image. In either case we do not see the human being who carries a projection for us as he or she actually is, because that person appears to us in the light of the projection.

When a woman projects her positive animus image onto a man she becomes greatly drawn to him. He appears fascinating to her, and her mind may become filled with fantasies about him. We call such a state "being" or "falling in love." To be in love means to have someone in our lives who carries the projected animus or anima image. Such a state can be beneficial in many ways. When we are in love, powerful emotions are released in us, and we are transformed by our experience. We are also drawn into a relationship with the person with whom we are in love, which sets life in motion. On the other hand, there are negative effects as well, for when a relationship is founded largely on projection it is an unconscious relationship, and cannot last long in that particular form. Sooner or later the human reality of our partner will emerge, and the projection will fall away. When this happens there may be great disillusionment or disappointment. The person who carries a projection also may begin to feel uncomfortable. A man who carries a woman's positive animus begins to feel that the relationship is getting sticky, and he stiffens and wants to draw away. A woman who carries a man's projected anima image is at first, as a rule, flattered by the attention that she receives and the sense of power, but if the relationship becomes permanent she soon begins to feel suffocated and confined, for a man in this state of mind does not want his woman to become an individual but to remain a personification of his anima.

Because the relationship of being in love is so unconscious, there are powerful forces at work in us that seek to break the relationship. At this point a true human relationship may begin to develop. That is, the two people may begin to discover a basis in human reality for their being together, and to find who they actually are apart from the projections they have carried for each other. This is also a golden opportunity for a man or woman to discover his or her inner partner, the anima or animus. What was it that made the woman seem like a goddess, or made the man appear so much bigger than life? If a person is able to see that it was something within himself or herself that caused the other person to loom so large, the possibility can exist for a more direct, psychological relationship with the all-important figures of the anima and animus, and hence for a closer relationship to the unconscious and the process of individuation.

All of this psychological development is a potentiality for Marie. The starting point for her is to face her emotions, and dare to let them show, and this is what the dream is bringing out. If Marie could develop enough of a relationship with the professor to perceive the difference between him as a man, and the animus as an inner, numinous figure, the possibility would come about for a real relationship with both the outer and the inner man. The energy for this would come from her eros, from her capacity to love, and in the process her eros would become differentiated. Through a real relationship with this professor her capacity to love could become real, for love is only real when it is lived out with real human beings and not with inner figures and the fantasies they evoke. The fantasies that go through our minds are not to be taken for real human love, but as attempts of the inner figures of the anima and animus to get our attention, and also, perhaps, as nature's way of drawing man and woman together into the maelstrom of relationship.

We have to ask to what extent this dream represents an accomplished fact and to what extent it represents a possible line of development. To a certain extent it is fact. Marie has not gone far in her relationship with the professor, but she has at least exposed herself to her feelings. She is no longer sitting at home with her secret thoughts writing notes to him. Now she sees him in the flesh and talks to him and faces up to her feelings for him. So she has, to a certain extent, lifted the drape from her face. On the other hand, circumstances have combined to keep the relationship with the professor from becoming more than a friendship. Certainly Marie is not yet aware that there is another man, inside of her, whom she sees reflected back to her when she looks at the professor, and that it is this man within who gives her great strength and guidance in her task of living a whole life. So to this extent the dream is not yet lived out. It represents a chart or map, as it were, showing the way she is to go, but it does not describe an accomplished psychological process.

Dream 2

Marie's second dream was as follows:

> "The dreamer was following a small white cat down a long, dark tunnel. It was a pet who had wandered away, which was why, despite an overpowering fear, she kept on. The darkness was so intense that it seemed to absorb the light from a small flashlight she carried. Despite the fact that the tunnel was so small she could have reached out and touched the sides, they could barely be distinguished in the darkness. The sides and roof were of rough-cut stone, quite damp.

Suddenly the cat appeared; running in terror it passed her without seeing her. She knew the animal was being chased by another creature. In her terror she dropped the light and pressed against the wall. It was so cold it penetrated through her clothes until it was impossible to tell the external cold from her fear. A huge black animal raced by her, in form and size similar to a black panther. It passed her without even a glance in her direction. She woke so terrified and cold she was unable to sleep for the remainder of the night."

Like the first dream, this one was so intense that it had a powerful effect on Marie. We can assume from this that the unconscious is trying to "stick" to her in order to expand her awareness of herself. As we have seen, when dreams are unusually beautiful, intense, or when they use color, it is as though they are making an unusual effort to be recognized by consciousness and to adhere to it so as to alter and affect oui state of mind. Naturally, we cannot say to what extent there is an intelligence within us that lies behind the dreams and "intends" such things. But nature does have her own intentions, and when we analyze our dreams it is wise to think about the unconscious as though it were exactly as purposeful as it appears to be, for this leads to the best results.

The dream begins with the plight of the little white cat that has wandered into this long, dark tunnel. Animals in dreams are suggestive of the instincts, the entirely natural part of us. Our conscious attitude is often at variance with the instincts. The price of civilization has been a cleavage between our conscious personality and the natural man. A wild animal always acts exactly as it is supposed to, a perfect representation of what the Creator had in mind, but we do not always act as we were meant to because our conscious minds, with their false ideals and egocentricity, get in the way. The result is anxiety, tension, and neurosis, for it is like being turned against oneself. For this reason, being on good terms with the animals in our dreams is very important; it means coming to terms with our instinctive nature and our natural self.

This is reflected in fairy tales. Many fairy tales begin with the miller and the miller's daughter. A certain miller has a daughter and, as the story develops, this daughter gets into trouble as a result of her father's activity. The miller is an early mechanic or technician, a man who harnesses nature to work for man's ego purposes. The result is damage to the daughter, to the natural, feminine spirit. When the ego developed out of pure nature it was a great boon, giving additional scope to man's conscious personality, but it was also a violation of nature, and damaged something within us. Similarly, we find in fairy tales that when the hero is on good terms with the animals in the story they come through at the end and play a saving role, enabling him to overcome the evil powers in a way that would have been impossible without them.

The fact that the cat is a pet tells us that a certain amount of instinct has become related to consciousness. Its whiteness suggests its purity, and its adaptation to conscious values. We can think of this little white cat as the instinct to give and receive affection, since that is the reason most people have cats. But the cat has wandered away, and although we do not know why, the effect of this is to involve Marie in a frightening adventure.

Bravely, Marie goes in search of her cat, even though the way leads through a long, dark tunnel. Fortunately she has a little flashlight in her hands that helps her in her overpowering fear of the darkness. Light is a symbol for consciousness. Since consciousness is a supreme spiritual value, light is used as a symbol in religious lore the world over for the attainment of a development of great importance. The Gospel of John stresses the importance of light over and over again, beginning, in the famous Prologue, with the words about the coming of the Logos as life, and "that life was the light of men, a light that shines in the dark, a light that darkness could not overpower."[1] We also have many sayings of Jesus in the Synoptic Gospels in which light is used as a symbol for conscious awareness. Jesus declared, "The lamp of the body is the eye. It follows

---

[1]John 1:5.

that if your eye is sound, your whole body will be filled with light. But if your eye is diseased, your whole body will be all darkness. If then, the light inside you is darkness, what darkness that will be!"[2] In Marie's case, her psychological consciousness is like the little light from the flashlight; it is not much, but in a dark tunnel it is a great blessing. Its importance cannot be overestimated, for man's greatest fear is of the darkness, and this extends to psychological matters as well. As long as we have no light, no psychological knowledge, we are bound to be afraid of the unconscious and its strange inner world, for we fear, with some justification, that we might become overwhelmed by what we do not see and so cannot understand. A little light on the mat- ter, made possible by some self-knowledge, changes all of this. Our fears can subside and we can begin to understand that the unconscious can also be our friend.

The tunnel is characteristically a symbol for rebirth. We all entered into this world by going through a tunnel—the birth canal. Picture yourself going through a long, dark tun- nel. You go and go and finally, eventually, you near the other end, and suddenly you step out of the tunnel and into the light on the other side. It is like being born again. This may be why the little white cat is in this tunnel: instinct seeks the light on the other side, the light of rebirth.

Rebirth is what Marie needs. She came to see me in the first place because of her hunger for a new life, and returned to school because of her urge for a larger life. These were the outer representations of a powerful movement within her for renewal. Individuation is a process of continual, often painful rebirth, hence the significance of Jesus' statement to Nicodemus, "I tell you most solemnly, unless a man is born from above, he cannot see the kingdom of God."[3] The tun- nel is extremely narrow; Marie can reach out and touch either side. This narrowness suggests anxiety, for the nar- row way is the anxious way. It is also the way of individua- tion. Jesus says about this, "Enter by the narrow gate, since the road that leads to perdition is wide and spacious, and

---

[2]Matt. 6:22.
[3]John 3:2.

many take it; but it is a narrow gate and a hard road that leads to life, and only a few find ⁺ "⁴

It takes a certain amount of courage for Marie to persevere down that tunnel in search of her little white cat. One must want something badly to face such fears as the tunnel contains, which suggests that she has a considerable amount of motivation to become whole, for even though her journey through the tunnel is not undertaken consciously for the sake of wholeness, that is what it represents. Without a certain motivation of the soul toward wholeness the individuation process cannot be accomplished, which is why no one else can do it for us. We must follow our own instinct wherever it leads us, and through whatever dangers might arise.

Partway through the tunnel Marie is startled to see her cat race past her, and she realizes it is being pursued by another animal. In her great terror she drops the light, that is, surrenders what little consciousness she has, and presses against the wall. Then the large, black panther-like creature races by her.

The blackness and size of the panther are in sharp contrast to the whiteness of the little cat. This is no tame kitty, but a fierce, wild, and natural being. Small wonder Marie is so terrified at the appearance of such a creature straight from mother nature, its wild heart not softened by contact with the human world. But she need not have been afraid, for the great cat races past her without so much as a glance. The unconscious powers in her do not intend the destruction of the ego, for the unconscious needs the ego if wholeness is to be realized. It is not her ego that must be destroyed, but her innocence and naïvete.

We can take the black panther as a symbol of Marie's own wild, instinctual nature, her sexuality, a part of herself to which she is almost totally unrelated. Its blackness means that it is still rooted in the unconscious and has little relationship to consciousness. It is like the black horse in Plato's famous allegory of the black and white horses that together

---

⁴Matt. 7:13.

drive the chariot of the soul, the one (the white horse) controlled and led by the driver, the other (the black horse) always pulling wildly in the opposite direction. This black panther is frightening, for its blackness suggests sin and the devil to our wary Christian consciences, but it cannot help but arouse our admiration for it appears to be a magnificent, vital creature, and filled with energy. And while the black panther has all the moral ambiguity of nature, it is not identical with evil, but is a pure manifestation of nature, and represents a great energy for living that Marie has within her.

The dream ends at this point of intense fear, because the unconscious can carry things no further. It is clear that Marie's individuation will require that she come to terms with everything in herself that the black panther represents, which will mean overcoming her anxiety about her own instinctual nature. Whether or not she does this will be up to Marie, which is the reason the dream ends where it does. As an unfinished dream it invites continuation through the technique of active imagination, though in this case the fear is so great it is doubtful if Marie could have come closer to the dream and its meaning without the assistance of another person to be a guide and companion along her way.

The first dream was friendly and inviting. It showed the positive, helpful nature of the unconscious and was a clear invitation to her to accept the unconscious as a partner; also an assurance that it would become a friend to her as she sought to become herself. This dream is not so inviting. It shows the frightening things she must face if she is to change. But it is not in any way a discouraging dream. It is Marie's fear that stands in the way of her development, not the unconscious. However, hard work lies ahead if this development is to take place, which is clear in the dream that follows.

Dream 3

Marie began this dream with the comment, "This is the shortest of the dreams."

"There was no movement and nothing or anyone else present. The dreamer was alone in the hall of an empty, small apartment. The entire floor, and halfway up the walls of every surface, was covered with excrement. The stench was overpowering, it could even be tasted. The dreamer was aware that she was to clean up the entire apartment. She woke before a move was made, and was still aware of the odor and nauseated."

There is no action in this dream; it is simply a scene. But it has a powerful impact on Marie who awakens with the nauseating scent so strong that it amounts to a kind of olfactory hallucination. Clearly the dream wants to make a deep impression upon her, and to convey the message: "There is a great, difficult, and repugnant task that you must undertake."

Individuation, becoming whole, *is* a *work*; it does not happen by chance or accident. To become whole we must carry whatever burden life has placed upon us, we must assume courageously the fate that has been dealt to us, and with the help of religion, psychology, and powers of self-reflection, strive for self-knowledge. This task now awaits our dreamer.

The dream describes the great task confronting Marie in very specific symbolism: it is like cleaning up the excrement that is all over the walls of the dreamer's living space. The dream might have chosen many ways to show her that a great task was ahead of her, but it selected this one particular symbol for some special reason of its own. So we have to ask why the symbol of the excrement was chosen by the dream.

We think of excrement as waste material of the body, as the lowest-of-the-low, as something filthy and repelling, something we do not want to get our hands into. From this point of view, it seems that the dream is telling Marie she must put her hands into the lowest, most repelling part of herself and clean it up. Among other things, this means she must become conscious of her shadow personality.

But Marie, we will recall, has lived an exemplary life. She has never done anything wrong; she has avoided sins and mistakes, and has been careful to live on the correct side of the Christian law. If anyone has led a pure life it is Marie, and now this dream is telling her that there is a terrible mess that she must clear up! That Marie has led a pure life is, however, a judgment from the conscious point of view. The dream expresses the unconscious, hence compensatory point of view. From the other end of the telescope, that is from the point of view of the unconscious, her life looks quite different. Looked at from the unconscious it is a mess, and she must get her hands into it.

The mess comes about because Marie has not become herself, and has not lived her own life. She has been so good and pure that she has hardly lived at all. Unlike the woman in Luke's Gospel, who washed Jesus' feet with her tears and dried them with her hair,[5] she has nothing to be forgiven for; therefore she has everything to be forgiven for. She is like the man in Jesus' parable who took his talent and buried it in the ground so it would be safe.[6] Marie has played it safe, so safe that life has not been lived, and this creates a terrible mess within her. She can no longer afford the kind of purity she has so carefully cultivated. Now, says the dream, she must get her hands into the mess, become soiled with her own self, and know what a child of the earth she is.

But excrement is not only waste to be washed away, it is also a kind of creative material. As any farmer knows, manure of any kind is an excellent fertilizer. In places like China human excrement is not flushed away, it is carried to the fields and spread over them so the crops will grow. There is also the fascination that we have all had, at least at one time, with excrement. As little children a bowel movement was a source of wonder and amazement. It can be said to be the first thing we could produce out of ourselves at will. For these reasons, excrement is often used in dreams to symbolize the kind of psychological material that the unconscious is always producing, which for the most part we flush away and disregard, but which in fact contains a sort of

---

[5]Luke 7:36-50.
[6]Matt. 25:14-30.

growing power for our lives. Our dreams and fantasies are
exactly like this. Most of us disregard these spontaneous
products of the unconscious. We pay no attention to them
and simply get rid of them. But if we cultivate the field of
our souls by deliberately paying attention to our dreams and
fantasies, things in us begin to grow.

So when our dreams come up with the earthy symbolism of the need for a bowel movement, or the presence of
excrement, it often represents our need to pay attention to
the spontaneous products of the unconscious, that is, our
dreams and fantasies. No matter how objectionable these
may seem to be, we need to get our hands into them. In
Marie's case, this would certainly include the love fantasies
she has for the professor, which have been the source of so
much guilt. No doubt this also would include various un-
welcome thoughts about her husband, spontaneous rumina-
tions about what she could do for a career, and any number
of other products of her imagination. Our minds are constantly filled with uninvited thoughts, images, desires, fantasies. To become whole we need to examine these, and
recognize that everything that finds its way into our screen
of consciousness has its origin in the unconscious, and has
been made conscious for a reason. Examining these things,
even if they seem objectionable, is part of the road to self-
knowledge.

Excrement is also a symbol of self-expression. As mentioned before, the child finds his bowel movement the first
thing that he can consciously produce out of himself. In a
dream, anything that comes out of the body may be used to
represent a creative urge. When we go to the bathroom it is
because we *have* to. There is a compelling urgency from
within that makes this earthy act an utter necessity. So this
is an apt symbol for the urge for self-expression that is in
each of us, and that also insists upon being obeyed. Looked
at from this point of view, Marie's dream is not only telling
her that she must look at what her life is; it is also telling her
that she can no longer waste her abundant creativity, but
must now follow her urge toward creative self-expression.

The task the dream poses her is enormous. We cannot

help but wonder if Marie can perform this work. Can it be done or is it beyond her power? There is a figure from Greek mythology who had much the same task laid upon him. Hercules, as one of his twelve great labors, had to clean out the stables of Aegeus, which had never been cleaned before, and so were filled with mountains of filth. His task looked insuperable, but the hero was able to perform it by diverting a river, which flowed through the stables and left them clean. So we have to hope that if Marie finds the hero archetype in herself the most difficult of psychological tasks will become possible for her.

It is important to note, however, that in this dream Marie has not yet begun this work. The dream ends with her simply sitting in the apartment aware of what she has to do. The dream specifies that she awakens "before a move was made." We must assume from this that the dream shows Marie what must now be done in her life, but that she has not yet reached a point of decision so that she can begin her individuation. In other words, the dream tells her what she must do; it also tells her that she has not yet begun. Like all the dreams in the series, this one is a map showing Marie where her growth process would take her, and inviting her to begin.

Dream 4

Marie's fourth dream, like the two before, was troubled:

> "The dreamer was filled with a hate so extreme she was shaking. She was standing in a richly furnished room facing a closed door. The door opened and a man entered. It was a man unknown to her when awake. As he came in she shot him and watched as he fell. He reached out one hand toward her and slowly she fired five more shots. It was obvious he was dead, but she kept pulling the trigger until the gun clicked empty. Each shot was deliberate and enjoyed. When the gun was empty she just stood and stared at him, still feeling the hatred, which slowly faded into exultation."

In this dream Marie faces something that she hates, and, apparently, destroys. The object of her hatred is a certain man, and so naturally we find ourselves asking who this man is and what he represents. The first thought that might come to our minds would be that the man whom she shoots with such evident satisfaction is her husband.

Here is a good illustration of the difference between the Freudian view of dreams and the Jungian view. The Freudian view would probably argue that the man whom she shot was indeed her husband, and that the dream was expressing her hatred of him and her desire to get away from him. True, the man was not identified in the dream as her husband, but this is only because such a thought would have been too objectionable to her Super Ego (that is, to her unconscious judge of what is right and wrong). The *manifest* dream content has the man who is killed an unknown man, but the *latent* meaning of the dream is that it is her husband, a fact the dream conceals because it seems too horrible to her that she should have such a thought.

The Jungian view says that dreams do not conceal anything, that they are products of nature, and the Spirit, and that nature does not lie. Therefore we must pay careful attention to *exactly what the dream says* or we are likely to go astray. The dream specifies that it "was a man unknown to her when awake." That makes it clear that this man is not her husband, but represents something in herself of which she knows little or nothing in her waking life.

The difference in the two ways of interpretation is obviously important. If the Freudian view were insisted upon by a therapist, Marie would be backed into a position in which she would either have to disagree resolutely with her analyst, or else would have to let herself be persuaded that she really did harbor such unconscious thoughts of hatred toward her husband. Needless to say, such a view would further disturb the relationship with her husband, which might be necessary if it were true that she had such bad feelings toward him, but would be destructive if she did not actually feel that way.

If the Jungian view is accepted, no such danger exists.

The Jungian attitude would be that if the dream meant to show that Marie has unconscious feelings of hatred toward her husband that she should pay attention to, it would have represented her husband in the dream. If the man in the dream is not her husband, but an unknown man, we are justified in wondering if this man is her animus, that is, the masculine part of herself of which she knows very little.

We have already discussed the fact that the animus has a positive and a negative aspect. We have seen the positive side in the first dream when the professor appeared as a helper and guide. This fourth dream portrays the negative animus. The animus is negative insofar as he is the voice of collective opinions that are not related to a woman's own psychological and emotional truth. When the animus functions this way, as we have seen, it is as though a woman carries around within herself a critical, judging, opinionated voice, which, upon analysis, turns out to be made up of an assortment of opinions from various authoritative sources such as parents, church, influential friends, etc. The animus is then experienced as autonomous thoughts that suddenly come into a woman's consciousness and talk to her: "You should do this. . . . You are a failure here. . . . What you are now is bad. . . . You have no right to want this or that. . . . " These are typical animus opinions, and they are like the devil when they go unexamined, for then a woman simply becomes identical with them. She then has no real mind of her own, but is a slave to what the animus says, and it is the animus who rules her life.

For most of her life Marie has been ruled by such a voice. She has not followed her own truth, but has done what the animus told her to do. She has not followed her heart, but has tried to conform her life to the opinions of the animus who told her what she "should" be like ("should" is the favorite word of the animus). Nor has she been true to her own thinking process, but has allowed the collective opinions of the animus to be a substitute for her own thinking. The result has been that a large part of her life for the last twenty years has been wasted. Small wonder she hates him so!

Hatred can be defined as "negative feeling." When we feel hatred we are beginning to separate ourselves from something or someone. This is why Jesus said, "If any man comes to me without hating his father, mother, wife, children, brothers, sisters, yes and his own life too, he cannot be my disciple."[7] What Jesus means is that we need to separate ourselves psychologically from precisely those people with whom we are naturally most identified so that we may become ourselves. In this sense, the hatred the dreamer feels toward the unknown man in her is a healthy reaction to an intolerable situation; i.e., her identification with and domination by the animus.

The gun that Marie has in the dream represents a certain amount of power at her conscious disposal. We can fire a gun at will; it is like an extension of our ego. In combating the animus Marie will need such ego strength. The negative animus and his opinions must be confronted, often with all the strength that a woman can muster, for he voices his opinions with an air of such authority that it takes a corresponding strength on the woman's part to confront him. Yet this is exactly what she must do. She must declare, "Why do you say that? Where does your authority for that come from? How can you say what I 'should' be doing? Where do you get the authority to run my life?" The battle with the negative animus is no easy task. Marie needs all the negative feeling she can muster to reinforce her, and give her the strength to overcome this tyrannical man within her who has dominated her for so long.

The fact that in the dream Marie seems to know this man, but does not know him when she is awake, is also an interesting point. We have already seen that the dream ego is both akin to the waking ego and different from it. Clearly this *is* Marie's ego in the dream doing the shooting. Yet we cannot entirely equate the figure of Marie in the dream with her conscious personality for when she is awake she does not know this man, though in the dream she knows him well enough to hate him. Apparently in her waking state Marie does *not* know about her negative animus. He has great

---
[7]Luke 14:26.

power over her precisely because she is unaware of him, and does not know how she becomes identical with his "shoulds" and judgments. So the dream anticipates a certain development in her. It is as though the dream is saying, "On a certain level you know about this man and what he is doing to you, and you must eventually take your stand against him as resolutely as you do in this dream."

Marie's exultation is also an important feature of this dream. To exult means literally "to leap vigorously." Killing the negative animus and his opinions is therefore a freeing act for Marie. She can now enter into life with renewed energy, for it is true that the negative animus has a paralyzing, draining effect on a woman's energy. He leaves her without life's color, and turns everything pale and cold.

The four dreams we have considered so far have given us a sweeping picture of what it will mean for Marie to become whole. She must face her feelings, even though they seem shameful, and have the courage to do without her mask. She must face those instincts within herself that frighten her so badly. She must clean up the mess in her life and have the ego strength to confront many unpleasant things about herself. And, finally, she must struggle with the negative animus and his defeating power. What might be the result of such a great psychological effort? The final dream in the series gives us a clue.

Dream 5

Marie's fifth dream:

"This was the longest and most detailed of the dreams. The dreamer had just had a child, a girl. She was in an elaborate dressing gown lying on a window seat. Outside the window was a beautiful garden, informal, in a tropical style, with large trees and a small stream. The dreamer knew that the house was in the city although no evidence of it could be seen. She was waiting for the man who was the father of her child. He was not her husband. She saw him enter the garden and come toward the house. She called a small, pleasant, older woman to take him the child and tell him, because she was afraid to face him. There was a short space of time when she could hear the sounds from the garden and the murmur of the water. He came into the room, carrying the baby. It was the same older man who was in the first dream. He put the child in her arms and said, 'You may name her whatever you like, but I shall call her Bonnie, because she is the gift of le bon Dieu.' The emotion that overwhelmed her was one of complete ecstasy as she held the child and looked up at the father. He stood smiling down at her and put his arm around them both. The emotion of this dream lasted for over an entire day."

The dream begins with a description of the setting: her dressing gown, her reclining posture, the informal, tropical garden, the small stream, a warm, natural *temenos* set in the middle of a city. It is a feminine scene, a scene of the earth and her gifts, a picture of *Yin*. It is as though the dreams want to bring Marie to her own deep, moist, dark, rich, creative *Yinness*. This has been the side of life that the negative animus of the previous dream has prevented her from living.

Then it appears that a child has been born, a baby girl. Of course a child is the birth of new life, so the dream is saying that a new life has been born in Marie, or, rather, that it can be born. When people start becoming whole they often dream of babies and children, for painful though individuation is (as we have seen in the previous three dreams), it ultimately brings the marvellous gift of a rich development. The child is an archetypal image, the image of a newborn wholeness, hence, the numinosity and emotional power of the story of the birth of the Christ child.

Usually in our dreams when a baby is born no one knows who the father is. It is an interesting feature of such dreams that not only do we seldom know the father of the child, but it seldom occurs to us to ask. This is because the father of the child, the one whose seed has germinated the new birth, is the creative activity of the unconscious itself. This is reflected in the biblical story in which the Christ child is fathered by the Holy Spirit and not by an ordinary mortal man. But in this dream the father is specified. It is the same older man who appeared in the first dream, that is, the professor, who, as we have seen, personified the creative functioning of the unconscious.

In the first dream there was some question whether the professor represented the actual professor with whom she was in love, or the inner creative man. There can be no doubt in this dream, for the actual professor has not fathered any such child within her, nor has their relationship reached the point where it could be said that he had started such a movement within her. The professor in the dream is her own positive, creative spirit, the guide and companion of her soul on its journey through life, the positive counterpart to the negative animus figure of the previous dream.

There is an ancient Babylonian tradition that at birth each soul is assigned two gods and two goddesses. One god and one goddess stand in defense of the soul and help it on its way; the other god and goddess attack the soul, accuse it, and do their best to keep it from making it successfully through life. A parallel to this belief is also found in Zechariah, chapter three, in which Joshua stands before a helping angel on one side and an accusing satan on the other, the angel clothing Joshua in new raiment, and satan standing ready to destroy him with accusations if he can. In actual life this is the way it appears to be. It is as though each of us carries an accusing, destructive voice or mood within us that acts for all the world as though it wants to destroy us, but also we have within us a helping power, an Advocate, as John's Gospel says, who is our counselor and our guide during life's journey.

There is a hint of the old shame in the dream in the fact that the dreamer is afraid to face the man with their child. But it no longer matters. The child has been born, and the residue of shame that she feels no longer stands in the way. So the pleasant, older woman, who is, perhaps, a represen-

tative of Demeter, ancient mother of all life, takes the baby
to the man.

Now the man enters carrying the infant girl, and with
great tenderness hands the child back to Marie with the
beautiful statement that he will call the child Bonnie, because she is the gift of the good God. We have seen what
dark and troubling experiences Marie would have to
undergo if she were to become whole: facing the black
panther, cleaning up the excrement, confronting the
dangerous man; these were dark and hazardous experiences. But behind all of this struggle and darkness, suggests
this dream, is God, Who has a great gift to give Marie: the
gift of wholeness and new life. Small wonder that as the
dream closes Marie is transported into ecstasy, and that the
dream left her with a powerful emotion that lasted throughout the day.

To be in ecstasy means to be out of oneself. As long as
we are locked within our boxlike egos we cannot experience
wholeness. When we see things only from the perspective of
the ego, we see everything separately, and experience
reality as a series of disparate entities; we perceive this or
that, but we miss the whole. In order to experience the inex-
pressible wholeness of life, called Tao in ancient Chinese
lore, or the Self in Jung's psychological language, or God in
Christian tradition, we must be lifted out of our egos and
apprehend the mystery of the incredible wholeness of all
things. So to become whole is to go beyond one's ego
boundaries, to experience a much larger reality than the
meagre world of consciousness. Ecstasy is a hallmark of all
great religious experiences that lift man beyond his usual
confinements, and place him in the middle of a much
greater reality.

Ecstasy is, of course, not a state in which we can remain
permanently. We are fortunate if we experience it from time
to time. Then, just as as flash of lightening illuminates the
sky for a moment, only to have the darkness close in again,
so after our moment of ecstasy, once again we are plunged
back into the ordinary world. But we do not forget what we
have seen. For a moment we were whole; for a flash we

stepped into reality. We cannot remain there, but we can remember that there is something beyond the usual world in which we live, and that the greater reality of wholeness is the mighty background against which life is played out.

As mentioned before, these dreams were never brought by Marie for analysis and discussion; they were a promise and an invitation.

After these dreams, Marie continued her studies and in a year or so graduated from the program. Unfortunately, there was no work available for her in the city in which she lived, and, to complicate matters further, her husband's health further deteriorated so that he was increasingly dependent upon her. Marie could not find work, nor could she bring herself to uproot her husband to search elsewhere for it. Therefore she has not yet utilized her training and skills except on an occasional basis.

As for her relationship with the professor, it too was not fulfilled—at least not as an outer relationship. She parted from him good friends, but not lovers, nor did he know to the end of her work with him how deeply she felt. Just the same, something happened to her as a result of her feelings for him. Her feelings had not been fully expressed, but they had become conscious to her and she had dared to let herself have them. Without realizing it, this professor had played a much greater role in her life than that of teacher to student.

Even though the dreams were not analyzed at the time, and the outer circumstances of Marie's life were not changed that much, the dreams did initiate a time of great inner change. A process of inner development did begin in Marie at the time of these dreams. It was somehow vital to her that she complete her graduate work; it helped her self-image to know she could do it. However, it also seemed to be her only choice to remain loyal to her husband, her affection for him, and his needs. In her own way, her personality began to unfold.

Life has many twists and turns, and each of us has a destiny to follow and fulfil that is like a thread that weaves its way in and out of all that happens to us. Our dreams help us find and follow this thread. We need this help, for otherwise the way is easily lost. When we lose the thread the dreams tell us that we have gone off the path. When we have found the thread the dreams tell us which way the path now turns. As the American Indians said, our dreams are like a guiding light given by the Great Spirit to souls that otherwise would wander in darkness. Now we can better understand Tertullian's comment quoted earlier: "Beyond a doubt the great part of mankind derive their knowledge of God from their dreams."[8] and that "from the beginning the knowledge of God is the dowry of the soul.[9]

---

[8]Tertullian, *A Treatise on the Soul*, Ch. XLVII.
[9]Tertullian, *Against Marcion*, Ch. X.

INDEX

Inasmuch as the principal subject in this book is dreams, that word is not included in the index; it appears on almost every page.

A

abaton, 108
Abraham Lincoln, The War Years, 6n
accident, 35, 86, 99, 105, 141
active imagination, 45, 59, 59n, 60, 61, 87, 140
adventure(s), 5, 52, 90, 92, 137
adversary, 47, 104
affect(s), 8, 15, 61
Against Marcion, 153n
'Aha!'', 21, 54
alchemists, 101
alcohol(ic)(ism), 9, 13, 22, 30, 35, 67
Alcoholics Anonymous, 22, 23
Alexander the Great, 91
Altered States of Consciousness, 66n
American Indian(s), 6, 13, 67, 73, 82, 83, 109-110, 153
angel(s), 6, 61, 103, 104, 105, 150
anger, 39, 61, 103, 104, 105
androgynous, 43
anima, 43, 78, 132, 133, 134, 135
animal(s): 103, 137; in dreams, 18, 25, 30, 32, 41, 136, 139
animus: and fantasies, 135; Jung's term, 43, 131; personification of masculine qualities, 131; positive and negative, 131, 134, 146, 147, 148, 149, 150; numinous archetype, 131; in projections, 132, 133, 134
anxiety: 107, 127, 138, 140; and conscious mind, 136; dark side of Self, 105; lack of sleep, 9; and nightmares, 46; and the unconscious, 33, 61, 106

Aphrodite, 120
archetype(s): 16, 17, 18, 50, 72, 131; collective unconscious, 17, 84; creative, 93; hero, 144; Jung's term, 16, 131; numinous, 25, 131; patterns, 16, 17, 43, 50; possessed by, 50; puer and senex, 77; sun as symbol, 84; wise old man, 82; projections, 133
arrogance, 102, 115, 116, 117
Asklepius, 14, 34, 108
attitude(s): 50, 118, 132; in active imagination, 60; change of, 46, 49, 79; childish, 73; collective, 50, 96; conscious, 17, 46, 50, 57, 79, 136; correct, 34, 40, 60, 76, 115; in dreams, 41, 46, 48, 49, 57, 86, 89, 101; and hybris, 102; individual, 51; Jungian, 146; materialistic, 7, 120; negative, 102, 111, 112, 113; nihilistic, 36; and power, 65; religious, 88, 119; and the unconscious, 17
Aztec(s), 27, 28, 83

B

Balaam, 103, 104, 105
bathroom, 22, 79, 143
baby(ies), 25, 149, 151
Bible, 6, 7, 8, 15, 25, 61, 84, 102, 109
body(ies): 16, 17, 35, 43, 44, 82, 99; of a church, 99; in dreams, 26, 30, 31, 114, 143; excrement of, 141; the lamp of, 137, 138; in meditation, 57; senses of, 8, 18
Bronte, Emily, 56, 56n
bullet(s), 24, 119, 121

C

Campbell, Joseph, 118
cancer, 35

case histories (also see Sanford, John A. - Cases), 2
Casting Director, 43, 44
causality, 46
center/Center: 55, 76; alchemical, 101; and dreams, 6, 20, 22, 24, 34, 43, 102, 119; ego-Self axis, 37, 38; inner, 19, 20; psychic, 28, 37, 38, 39; and the unconscious, 37
change(s): 8, 56, 67, 119, 120, 121, 123; of attitude, 46, 49, 79; in consciousness, 46; and dreams, 39, 46, 56, 105, 109, 114, 152; and individuation, 20; psychological, 31, 78
Chief Joseph, 83
Chief Seattle, 6, 83
child/children: 26, 100, 110, 111, 112, 125, 142, 143, 149, 150; Chief Seattle quotation, 83; and dreams, 31, 32, 33, 47, 65, 70, 72, 76, 77, 78, 148, 149, 150, 151; Luke quotation, 147, 14:26, 147n; and parents, 71, 73, 74, 75, 93; puberty rites, 74; St. Christopher Legend, 62
childhood, 24, 51, 71, 73, 113
Children of Sanchez, The, 26, 27n
choice(s), 70, 71, 79, 90, 95, 97, 98, 122, 152
Choice Is Always Ours, The, 122n
Christ, 24, 28, 62, 83, 88, 109, 149, 150
Christian(ity): 8, 109, 113, 120
Christopher, 62
church: 5, 8, 23, 92, 106, 117, 120, 123, 146; early, 7, 13, 99; Christian, 7, 13, 120; Fathers of, 7, 88; Mother, 110, 112; rituals of, 85; Roman Catholic, 112
circulatio, 101
compensation, 39, 78, 81, 83, 100
conflict(s), 32, 35, 36, 55, 90, 91, 125, 127
conscience(s), 23, 86, 90, 127, 140
consciousness: 15, 16, 20, 50, 55, 60, 92, 116, 119, 130, 132, 138, 143, 146, 151; and archetypes, 16, 17, 50; changes in, 20, 46, 56; and dreams, 3, 19, 33, 34, 37, 39, 44,

46, 47, 56, 57, 64, 80, 87, 90, 91, 119, 121, 123, 136, 137, 139; ego, 43; and instinct, 137; masculine/feminine, 84; REM sleep, 9; thoughts of, 18; and the unconscious, 34, 37, 44, 58, 87
Consuelo, 26, 27, 28, 33
courtroom scene, 59
conveyances in dreams, 99-101
Creative Dreaming, 44
creature(s)/creatureliness, 7, 18, 25, 34, 48, 88, 136, 139, 140
crime, 7, 67

D

danger(s): 27, 33, 53, 87, 93, 113, 114, 115, 128, 139, 145; in active imagination, 61; and heroes, 36, 93; and the unconscious, 36, 101; of hybris, 114
Daniel, 14, 15, 18, 19, 20, 21
Daniel, Book of, 12; 2:4, 14n; 2:30, 15n; 21n
darkness: 61, 121, 135, 137, 138, 151; Jesus' quotation, 138; powers of, 28, 121; and the soul, 6, 153; The Tempest, 42
Dark Speech of the Spirit, 7n
dawn, 27, 69, 76, 84
death, 6, 31, 32, 73, 108, 109, 114, 120
delerium tremens, 9
Demeter, 151
depression, 36, 39, 48, 106
depth(s), 1, 11, 13, 16, 81, 82, 90, 112, 126; depth psychology, 9, 56
destiny, 152
development: 11, 16, 17, 36, 43, 47, 50, 77, 87, 109, 113, 121, 131, 135, 137, 140, 148, 149; child's, 32; and the devil, 122; dreams, 25, 45, 48, 91; and ego, 42, 48; and growth, 11, 39, 97n; inner, 122, 123, 152; masculine, 77; and personality, 25; psychological, 47-48, religious, 85; spiritual, 81
devil(s) (also see Satan), 61, 66, 67, 104, 119, 120, 122, 140, 146
Dionysius, 120

house(s): 67, 81, 97n, 111, 125; in dreams, 18, 30, 49, 56, 69, 70, 72, 76, 78, 79, 94, 95, 148, 149; in fantasy, 60; inner, 22, 23; Jesus' parable, 95
Huitzilopochtli, 27, 83
hybris (also see inflation), 102, 114, 115, 116

I

I Ching, The, 115
idea(s): 1, 2, 49, 55, 65, 92, 100, 115, 133; archetypes, 16; consciousness, 18; dreams, 30, 56, 62, 63, 66, 101; Freud's revolutionary, 10, 11; Jungian psychology, 66; and the unconscious, 34; Wuthering Heights, 56
Idea of the Holy, The, 25n, 88n
inflation (also see hybris), 102
ill(s)/illness: 7, 10, 30, 31, 35, 51, 67, 81, 105, 125; diagnosis via dreams, 30; shamans, 109
image(s)/imagery: 143, 152; and active imagination, 61, 87; and anima/animus, 78, 132, 133, 134; and the archetypes, 16, 82, 149; Christian, 119; and the collective unconscious, 16, 82, 112; of death and renewal, 109; and dreams, 12, 18, 33, 34, 36, 39, 44, 45, 48, 57, 58, 63, 65, 83, 84, 95, 101, 102, 109, 116; Eastern, 118; feminine, 112; of the inner world, 14, 113; in meditation, 57; of ourselves, 42; projections, 132, 133, 134; Wholeness, 149; and the unconscious, 18, 34, 60, 109
Indian(s)/Indian Chief: 82, 83; and active imagination, 87; Chief Joseph, 83; Chief Seattle, 6, 83; and dreams, 80, 81, 82, 84, 85, 86, 87, 89, 114; Jung on the Indian and the American psyche, 82
individuation: 88, 118, 131, 134, 138, 140, 141; anima/animus help, 131, 134; changes required, 20; circulatio, 101; and dreams, 20, 25, 32, 128, 140, 144, 149; needs a strong ego, 115; and

Eros, 130; fundamental instinct, 18; Jung's term, 18; process of rebirth, 138; wholeness, 139
Inner World of Childhood, The, 33
insight(s), 3, 21, 50, 51, 63, 64, 116
instinct(s)/instinctuality, 16, 18, 32, 91, 92, 136, 137, 138, 139, 148
Interpretation of Dreams, The, 9

J

Jacob, 61
James, William, 14
Jesus: active imagination, 61; as a boy, 74, 75; in a dream, 114, 117, 119, 121; on the Mount of Transfiguration, 84; parables, 19, 76, 95, 116, 142; sayings, 1, 19, 47, 64, 67, 95, 115, 137, 138, 147; solitude for prayer, 13; and the rich, young ruler, 121, 122; the woman who washed His feet, 142; the temptations, 122
Job, 102
Job, Book of, 7:13-14, 33:14-18, 103n
John's Gospel, 137; 1:5, 137n; 3:2, 138n; 150
Johnson, Robert, 75n
Jonah, 96
Jonah, Book of, 96
Jones, Ernest, 10n
Joshua, 150
journey: 91, 94, 98, 107, 108, 139; for healing, 108, 109; life's, 150
Jung(ian), C. G.: 18; active imagination, 59, 59n; analyst, 55; anima/animus, 43, 78, 131; and archetypes, 16; autobiography, 2; the dragon, 36; and dreams, 11, 12, 30, 49, 88, 145, 146; and Freud, 9, 11, 15, 145; the hero in myths, 36; Indians and the American psyche, 82; individuation, 18; persona, 130; religere defined, 88; and the Self, 102, 151; Senoi Indians, 66; symbols, 63; tradition, 25; and the unconscious, 15, 97
Works: *The Interpretation of Visions* in Spring Magazine, 97n

Letters I, 102n
Letters II, 30n, 88n
Memories, Dreams, Reflections, 2
Tavistock Lectures, 59n, 83n
Visions Seminars, 63, 63n
CW 14, Mysterium Coniunctionus, 36n, 59n
CW 16, The Practice of Psychotherapy, 42n
CW 18, The Symbolic Life, 30n, 83n

K

Kelsey, The Rev. Morton T., 7, 7n, 57n
kingdom of heaven, 19, 76, 99
kingdom of God, 1, 138
Kirsch, James, 37, 37n
kitten people, 118
Kluger, Rivkah Sharf, 103n
knowledge: 2, 19, 20, 21, 28; absolute, 87; and dreams, 21, 25, 28, 41, 52, 85; of God, 6, 7, 20, 153; psychological, 138; puberty rites, 73; self-, 35, 132, 133, 138, 141, 143; spiritual, 75, 85
Kunkel, Fritz, 5

L

Laughter and Liberation, 90, 90n
Lewis, Oscar, 26, 27n
libido, 10
life, times to analyze it, to live it . . . 92
Life and Work of Sigmund Freud, The, 10n
Lincoln, Abraham, 6, 56
Logos, 137
love: 21, 113, 125, 126, 130, 134, 135; archetypal experience, 17; and dreams, 129; Eros, 130; heart symbol for, 109
Luke's Gospel, 17:21, 1n; 2:49, 74n; 9:29, 84n; 18:18-23, 121n; 7:36-50, 142; 142n; 14:26, 147n
Lucid Dreaming, Dawning of the Clear Light, 45n
lysis, 46, 49

Mc

McCluhan, T. C., 6n; 83n

M

"Man from Mars" game, 52
Mark's Gospel, 10:17-22, 121n
mask, 130, 148
Matthew's Gospel, 13:31, 19n; 5:25-26, 47n; Chapter 4, 61n; 7:6, 64n; 4:4, 67n; 76; 7:24-27, 95n; 10:39, 115n; 25:14, 116n; 19:16-22, 121n; 6:22, 138n; 7:13, 139n; 25:14-30, 142n
maturity, 73, 75, 77
meditation, 57, 57n, 58, 59, 118
mind(s): 12, 15, 29, 45, 51, 61, 76, 79, 91, 120, 122, 127, 136, 143; active imagination, 61; animus, 146; archetypal, 16; associations, 51, 52; Daniel, 15, 18; dialogues, 59; and dreams, 22, 63, 120, 136, 145; fantasies, 135; inner/unconscious, 15, 18; and meditation, 57; parable of the young ruler, 121; and projections, 133, 134; Wuthering Heights, 56, 119
Mindess, Harvey, 90, 90n
modesty, 115, 116
monkey people, 118
mood(s), 8, 55, 61, 160
moon/moonlight, 42, 73, 84
Moses, 84, 85, 96
mother: 31, 39, 73, 110, 112, 116, 118; and anima, 78; archetypal, 73, 112; church, 110, 112; complex, 77; Consuelo's, 26; Demeter, 151; and dreams, 39, 40, 108, 110, 113, 116; earth, 111; and emotion, 110; of God, 117; Great, 110, 112, 113; in the Holy Grail Legend, 75; Holy Mother Mary, 112; Jesus' quotation, 147; Martin's, 72, 110, 111, 112, 116; nature, 139; psychological, 112; and puberty rites, 74
mountain(s), 14, 18, 80, 83, 88, 106
Mount Sinai, 13, 84
Mount of Transfiguration, 84
mustard seed, 19

and the shadow, 42; Tertullian's quotation, 153

Sparrow, Gregory Scott, 45n

spirit(s): 11,49,65,83,114,122,132; in dreams, 80, 85, 86, 122, 145, 150; feminine, 137; Great-, 83, 85; the Holy-, 150; numinous, 24; puer/senex, 77, 78; of the Red Man, 83; symbol of air, 100

star(s), 27, 42, 132

Stevenson, Robert Louis, 47, 47n, 52, 52n, 56, 80

Stewart, Kilton, 65, 66, 66n

sun/sunlight, 27, 42, 73, 76, 80, 83, 84

Super Ego, 10, 145

symbol(s)/symbolism: 112; archetypal, 24, 26, 32, 63, 82, 90, 93, 109, 112; of Christianity, 109; and dreams, 11, 25, 28, 30, 52, 57, 58, 62, 63, 83, 84, 112, 139, 141, 143; feminine, 112; God, 83; and healing, 34; heart, 109; light, 137; medical, 34; meditation, 57; numinous, 88; psychological, 24, 96; rebirth, 138; religious, 25; of shamans, 109; sun, 83, 84; and the unconscious, 16, 18, 52, 101; of wholeness, 24

T

talents, parable of, 116, 142

Tao, 151

Tart, Charles T., 66n

temenos, 149

Tempest, The, 42, 42n

Temptations in the Wilderness, 61, 122

"tender-minded-visionaries," 14

Tertullian, 7, 7n, 21, 153, 153n

thinking, collective, 50

thinking, symbolic, 18, 19, 120

Thomson, The Rev. Richard D., 1

Thurston, Mark, 62n

Touch the Earth, 6n, 83n

"tough-minded-hunters," 14

tradition(s), 8, 25, 93, 113, 150, 151

Transfiguration, Mount of, 84

Treatise on the Soul, A., 7n, 21n, 153n

tree(s), 11, 18, 132, 148

truth(s), 5, 37, 61, 113, 146

U

unconscious, 1, 13, 14, 17, 18, 21, 33 35, 36, 45, 48, 55, 60, 67, 98, 102, 107, 117, 123, 131, 136, 138, 139 140, 142, 143, 150; and active imagination, 59, 61; ambivalent, 34; anger of, 105, 106; anima/animus, 43, 78, 134; Biblical synonym, 15; compensates, 36; and consciousness, 15, 33, 37, 44, 58, 87; dangerous side, 36, 49; destructive/healing, 34, 36, 40; and dreams, 3, 13, 15, 18, 28, 33, 34, 36, 37, 40, 44, 48, 51, 54, 55, 56, 60, 67, 80, 81, 82, 87, 91, 96, 101, 102, 109, 128, 136, 142; and the ego-Self axis, 37; and the ego, 56, 71, 117, 139; and energy, 36, 37, 57, 58, 60, 61; and fantasy, 60; fear of, 138; Freud and Jung, 15; the gods, 102; Jung quotation, 97; individuation, 18; language of, 18, 19, 21; mind, 15; as mother, 112; and projections, 132, 133; reflects face we turn toward it, 46, 66; religious, 88; water symbol of, 101

unconscious, collective: 15, 16, 17, 18, 112; archetypes, 17, 84; collective thinking, 50; dreams, 25, 28, 29, 32, 46, 52, 82; energy, 18; and the serpent, 34

unconscious, personal, 15, 16, 18, 29

V

value(s), 65, 67, 77, 88, 91, 92, 97, 137

"vessel for divine grace," 102

Vietnam, 72

vision(s), 6, 15, 73, 103

Vision Quest, 13, 73

voice(s): accusing, 59, 150; active imagination, 59, 60; animus, 146; autonomous, 59; collective, 96; and dreams, 12, 95, 96, 97

114, 117, 119, 121, 122; of God, 96; within, 5, 23, 60, 61, 126

W

war(s), 7, 24, 65, 67, 72
Wakan Tanka, 85
water(s): 1, 13, 63, 64; in dreams, 29, 39, 98, 101, 105, 106, 149; in puberty rites, 74; and the unconscious, 56, 101; Wuthering Heights, 56
whole/wholeness: 18, 37, 40, 78, 88, 108, 116, 118, 120, 128, 139, 141, 143, 148, 149, 151, 152; child an image of, 149; and dreams, 20, 53, 62, 84, 151; and the ego, 115, 118, 139; and energy, 11, 28; and eros, 130; God's plan for man, 18; and individuation, 139; psy-chological, 5, 24
Wickes, Frances, 33
Wilhelm, Richard, 115n
Will (God's), 96, 104, 115
wisdom, 5, 6, 17, 18, 21, 80, 81, 82, 84, 85
Wise Old Man, 82
Wolf, William J., 6n
World War II, 8, 24, 50
Wuthering Heights, 56, 56n, 119

Y

Yahweh, 103, 104, 105
Yang, 84
Yin, 84, 149

Z

Zechariah, 150